Bedside Companion
for Book Lovers

Bedside Companion for Book Lovers

EDITED BY JANE MCMORLAND HUNTER

BATSFORD

First published in the United Kingdom in 2022 by
B. T. Batsford Ltd
43 Great Ormond Street
London
WC1N 3HZ

An imprint of B. T. Batsford Holdings Ltd

ISBN 978 1 84994 769 5

A CIP catalogue record for this book is available from the
British Library.

10 9 8 7 6 5 4 3 2

Reproduction by Rival Colour Ltd, UK
Printed and bound by Toppan Leefung Printing Ltd, China

Illustrations by Elen Winata

CONTENTS

For Julie, book-reader, bookseller, book-buyer and friend,
and obviously for Matilda,
with all my love.

Acknowledgements

As always, a huge thank you to everyone at Hatchards for looking after my books so well. I could not have compiled this anthology without a great deal of help from friends including Julie Apps, Francis Cleverdon, Ryan Edgington, Sue and David Gibb, Sally Hughes, Louy and David Piachaud, Ian Prince, Kaaren Ramus, Freddie Rowe, Jack Ruddy, Flo Sandelson, Julia Schaper, Danny Stringer, Will Taylor and Georgia Williams. They suggested titles and researched entries for me – for which, many thanks. My editors at Batsford, Tina Persaud and Nicola Newman, make compiling these anthologies a true pleasure. Matilda, my small grey tabby cat, helps in a uniquely feline way; she acts as paperweight on anything I am trying to read, keeps the laptop warm by sleeping on it and forces me to type one-handed whilst stroking her.

About the editor

Jane McMorland Hunter has compiled ten anthologies for Batsford and the National Trust including collections on gardening, nature, friendship, London, England and the First World War. She has also worked as a gardener, potter and quilter, writes gardening, cookery and craft books and works at Hatchards Bookshop in Piccadilly. She lives in London in a small house overflowing with books.

Introduction

I grew up in a house full of books, have worked in bookshops for most of my adult life and now live in a house where the books regularly threaten to take over. My love of books, and stories in particular, began early; every night my parents read to me, although they chose the books, with the result that by the time I went to school I had a wide but fragmented knowledge of Charles Dickens's novels and was under the mistaken impression that P. G. Wodehouse wrote children's books about pigs. Looking round my shelves when I started collecting pieces for this anthology, I was slightly daunted. Three hundred and sixty-six extracts may seem a lot, but I soon realised that I would have a problem when I compiled a 'short'list of over 480 possibilities.

I have attempted to cover all aspects of books and the book world: books themselves, reading, writing, bookshops and libraries, both public and private. I have included pieces of historical interest, but this is not intended to give a comprehensive history of books; there are recommendations in the bibliography on 31 December for those who wish to delve deeper. Indeed, it is my hope that this collection will inspire readers to go off at tangents – either to reread a forgotten favourite or to explore a new discovery.

I started with the books themselves: bestsellers, dictionaries, biographies, diaries, short stories, fact and fiction. Of all the different types of book, it was fiction that divided opinion most. Novels were blamed for leading children into a life of crime and, for many years, were regarded as something one did not readily admit to reading. I found copious advice on what to read and how to make the most of your reading time; it was not until recently that it was widely admitted that you could simply read for fun.

Before you can make choices, of course, you need to learn to read, and while this is an accomplishment many take for granted, some of these extracts tell a very different story, with would-be readers having to resort to secrecy and subterfuge. Writers also have a part in this collection, giving both advice on how to write and explanatory pieces or 'arguments' and 'apologies' regarding their own works. Where to read and write also divides opinion: a large room, a small room, inside or out, all have their supporters.

I could not have complied this without including many pieces on bookshops – from owning a bookshop, to dealing with customers, to browsing for the perfect book. In contrast, online shopping has no mention although, perhaps, I did not look very hard. I have attempted to be unbiased but my favourite authors have inevitably been given preferential treatment, and as a result I have not provided a comprehensive overview of literature but rather a collection that dips and dives wherever I found something of interest. I have not judged the writers; there is literary criticism here, but equally there is criticism of the critics themselves.

The extracts are a mixture of fact, fiction, prose, poetry, adult's and children's books, ranging from Cicero to the present day. Some pieces link with their neighbours, following a theme for a few days' reading, while others stand alone, providing changes each day. There are biographical sketches giving brief glimpses of some authors and extracts from openings of some books, which we all know, but all too briefly. Everyone knows of the man who must be in want of a wife, the rarely quoted scene that follows is every bit as perceptive and entertaining.

There are, of course, as many omissions as inclusions, and many of the stories that I could not fit into the main anthology are clustered together on New Year's Eve; I feel one should always start the year with plenty of reading matter close to hand.

I have, of necessity, had to cut nearly all the entries from larger works but in all cases I have given the original source. Some authors have also had to be omitted for copyright reasons. My aim has been to create an anthology which will provide the reader with a little pleasurable bookishness for every day of the year and, if wanted, a route to following an author further. I hope you enjoy this collection.

JANUARY

An Illimitable Choice

The Use and Value of a Little Reading

From *The Uses of Reading, 1912* | Rudyard Kipling (1865–1936)

To the late Mr Pearson's House at Wellington College: May 1912

There is, or there was, an idea that reading in itself is a virtuous and holy deed. I can't quite agree with this, because it seems to me that the mere fact of a man's being fond of reading proves nothing one way or the other. He may be constitutionally lazy; or he may be overstrained, and so take refuge in a book to rest himself. He may be full of curiosity and wonder about the life on which he is just entering; and for that reason may plunge into any and every book he can lay hands on, in order to get information about things that are puzzling him, or frightening him, or interesting him.

Now, I am a very long way from saying that literature ought to be a chief or a leading interest in most men's lives, or even in the life of a nation. But a man who goes into life with no knowledge of the literature of his own country and without a certain acquaintance with the classics and the value of words, is as heavily handicapped as a man who takes up sports or games without knowing what has been done in these particular sports or games, before he came on the scene. He doesn't know the records and so he can't have any standards.

. . . .

Choosing:
That is just a question of temperament; and a man is no more to be blamed for not caring for certain forms of literature than he is for not thriving on certain forms of food.

Edward's Reading

From *Waverley, 1814* | Sir Walter Scott (1771–1832)

Chapter III: Education

The library at Waverley-Honour, a large Gothic room, with double arches and a gallery, contained such a miscellaneous and extensive collection of volumes as had been assembled together, during the course of two hundred years, by a family which had been always wealthy, and inclined, of course, as a mark of splendour, to furnish their shelves with the current literature of the day, without much scrutiny, or nicety of discrimination. Throughout this ample realm Edward was permitted to roam at large.

. . . .

[Edward] like the epicure who only deigned to take a single morsel from the sunny side of a peach, read no volume a moment after it ceased to excite his curiosity or interest; and it necessarily happened, that the habit of seeking only this sort of gratification rendered it daily more difficult of attainment, till the passion for reading, like other strong appetites, produced by indulgence a sort of satiety.

Ere he had attained this indifference, however, he had read, and stored in a memory of uncommon tenacity, much curious, though ill-arranged and miscellaneous information.

What to Read

From *The Private Library, 1897* | A. L. Humphreys (1865–1946)

Junior Assistant and later Partner, Hatchards Bookshop (1881–1924)

Be very careful about reading books which are recommended, because they are books of the hour. Fools step in and say read this and that without thinking to put themselves in your place. Because a book suits one person, it is only a rare chance that it will suit a friend equally.

Before recommending a book to another with assurance, you must know the book well, and the friend to whom it is recommended you must know much better. Read the book which suggests something responsive and sympathetic. No one can tell you this as well as you can find it for yourself. Practice will teach you to choose a book, as practice has taught you to choose a friend. You will almost be able to choose it in the dark. There are affinities for books as for people, but this does not come at once.

The proper appreciation of the great books of the world is the reward of lifelong study. You must work up to them, and unconsciously you will become trained to find great qualities in what the world has decided is great. Novel reading is not a part of the intellectual life, it is a part of the fashionable life.

3 January

Sonnet

William Wordsworth (1770–1850)

A poet! – He hath put his heart to school,
Nor dares to move unpropped upon the staff
Which Art hath lodged within his hand – must laugh
By precept only, and shed tears by rule.
Thy Art be Nature; the live current quaff,
And let the groveller sip his stagnant pool,
In fear that else, when Critics grave and cool
Have killed him, Scorn should write his epitaph.
How does the Meadow-flower its bloom unfold?
Because the lovely little flower is free
Down to its root, and, in that freedom, bold;
And so the grandeur of the Forest-tree
Comes not by casting in a formal mould,
But from its *own* divine vitality.

Dickens's Characters

From *The Reading of Books, 1946*

George Holbrook Jackson (1874–1948)

When appreciating a novel the reader passes through the emotional experiences not only of the author, but those also of the characters depicted. The more excellent the novel the more profound the experience. The whole English-speaking world passed through the emotional experiences of Dickens during the middle decades of the last century.

First Lines

From *David Copperfield, 1850* | Charles Dickens (1812–1870)

Whether I shall turn out to be the hero of my own life, or whether that station will be held by anybody else, these pages must show. To begin my life with the beginning of my life, I record that I was born (as I have been informed and believe) on a Friday, at twelve o'clock at night. It was remarked that the clock began to strike, and I began to cry, simultaneously.

In consideration of the day and hour of my birth, it was declared by the nurse, and by some sage women in the neighbourhood who had taken a lively interest in me several months before there was any possibility of our becoming personally acquainted, first, that I was destined to be unlucky in life; and secondly, that I was privileged to see ghosts and spirits; both these gifts inevitably attaching, as they believed, to all unlucky infants of either gender, born towards the small hours on a Friday night.

I need say nothing here, on the first head, because nothing can show better than my history whether that prediction was verified or falsified by the result. On the second branch of the question, I will only remark, that unless I ran through that part of my inheritance while I was still a baby, I have not come into it yet. But I do not at all complain of having been kept out of this property; and if anybody else should be in the present enjoyment of it, he is heartily welcome to keep it.

The Library

John Greenleaf Whittier (1807–1892)

Sung at the opening of Haverhill Library, November 11, 1875

'Let there be light!' God spake of old,
And over chaos dark and cold,
And, through the dead and formless frame
Of nature, life and order came.

Faint was the light at first that shone
On giant fern and mastodon,
On half-formed plant and beast of prey,
And man as rude and wild as they.

Age after age, like waves, o'erran
The earth, uplifting brute and man;
And mind, at length, in symbols dark
Its meanings traced on stone and bark.

On leaf of palm, on sedge-wrought roll,
On plastic clay and leathern scroll,
Man wrote his thoughts; the ages passed,
And to! the Press was found at last!

Then dead souls woke; the thoughts of men
Whose bones were dust revived again;
The cloister's silence found a tongue,
Old prophets spake, old poets sung.

And here, to-day, the dead look down,
The kings of mind again we crown;
We hear the voices lost so long,
The sage's word, the sibyl's song.

Here Greek and Roman find themselves
Alive along these crowded shelves;
And Shakespeare treads again his stage,
And Chaucer paints anew his age.

As if some Pantheon's marbles broke
Their stony trance, and lived and spoke,
Life thrills along the alcoved hall,
The lords of thought await our call!

Universe or Library?

From *The Library of Babel, 1941* | Jorge Luis Borges (1899–1986)

Translated by Andrew Hurley (1944–)

The universe (which other call the Library) is composed of an indefinite, perhaps finite number of hexagonal galleries. In the center of each gallery is a ventilation shaft, bounded by a low railing. From any hexagon you can see the floors above and below – one after another, endlessly. The arrangement of the galleries is always the same: Twenty bookshelves, five to each side, line four of the hexagon's six sides; the height of the bookshelves, floor to ceiling, is hardly greater than the height of a normal librarian. One of the hexagon's free sides opens onto a narrow sort of vestibule, which in turn opens onto another gallery, identical to the first – identical in fact to all. To the left and right of the vestibule are two tiny compartments. One is for sleeping, upright; the other, for satisfying one's physical necessities. Through this space, too, there passes a spiral staircase, which winds upward and downward into the remotest distance. In the vestibule there is a mirror, which faithfully duplicates appearances. Men often infer from this mirror that the Library is not infinite – if it were, what need would there be for that illusory replication? I prefer to dream that burnished surfaces are a configuration and promise of the infinite.

The Life of Books

From *Note-books, 1912* | Samuel Butler (1835–1902)

When a man is in doubt about this or that in his writing, it will often guide him if he asks himself how it will tell a hundred years hence.

. . . .

Some writers think about the life of books as some savages think about the life of men – that there are books which never die. They all die sooner or later but that will not hinder an author from trying to give his book as long a life as he can get for it. The fact that it will have to die is no valid reason for letting it die sooner than can be helped.

9 January

21

The Author's Apology for his Book

From *The Pilgrim's Progress, 1678* | John Bunyan (1628–1688)

When at the first I took my pen in hand
Thus for to write, I did not understand
That I at all should make a little book
In such a mode; nay, I had undertook
To make another; which, when almost done
Before I was aware, I this begun.

Bookplates

From *Gossip in a Library, 1891* | Edmund Gosse (1849–1928)

The outward and visible mark of the citizenship of the book-lover is his book-plate. There are many good bibliophiles who abide in the trenches, and never proclaim their loyalty by a book-plate. They are with us, but not of us; they lack the courage of their opinions; they collect with timidity or carelessness; they have no heed for the morrow. Such a man is liable to great temptations. He is brought face to face with that enemy of his species, the borrower, and dares not speak with him in the gate. If he had a book-plate he would say, 'Oh! certainly I will lend you this volume, if it has not my book-plate in it; of course, one makes a rule never to lend a book that has.' He would say this, and feign to look inside the volume, knowing right well that this safeguard against the borrower is there already. To have a book-plate gives a collector great serenity and self-confidence.

Two Distinct Races

From The Last Essays of Elia: Two Races of Men, 1823 |
Charles Lamb (1775–1834)

The human species, according to the best theory I can form of it, is
composed of two distinct races, *the men who borrow, and the men
who lend.* To these two original diversities may be reduced all those
impertinent classifications of Gothic and Celtic tribes, white men,
black men, and red men. All the dwellers upon earth, 'Parthians, and
Medes, and Elamites', flock hither, and do naturally fall in with one
or other of these primary distinctions. The infinite superiority of the
former, which I choose to designate as the *great race*, is discernible in
their figure, port, and a certain instinctive sovereignty. The latter are
born degraded. 'He shall serve his brethren.' There is something in
the air of one of this cast, lean and suspicious; contrasting with the
open, trusting, generous manners of the other.

. . . .

What a careless, even deportment hath your borrower! what rosy
gills! what a beautiful reliance on Providence doth he manifest,
– taking no more thought than lilies! What contempt for money, –
accounting it (yours and mine especially) no better than dross!
What a liberal confounding of those pedantic distinctions of *meum*
and *tuum*! or rather what a noble simplification of language.

The Bibliomania, An Epistle to Richard Heber, esq.

John Ferriar (1761–1815)

Lines 1–10

What wild desires, what restless torments seize
The hapless man, who feels the book-disease,
If niggard Fortune cramp his gen'rous mind,
And Prudence quench the Spark by heaven assign'd!
With wistful glance his aching eyes behold
The Princeps-copy, clad in blue and gold,
Where the tall Book-case, with partition thin,
Displays, yet guards the tempting charms within:
So great Facardin view'd, as sages tell,
Fair Crystalline immur'd in lucid cell.

Dusting and Rearranging

Andrew Lang (1844–1912)

Housemaids are seldom bibliophiles. Their favourite plan is to dust the books in the owner's absence, and then rearrange them on fancy principles, mostly upside down. One volume of *Grote* will be put among French novels, another in the centre of a collection on sports, a third in the midst of modern histories, while others are 'upstairs and downstairs, and in my lady's chamber'. The diversity of sizes, from folio to duodecimo, makes books very difficult to arrange where room is scanty. Modern shelves in most private houses allow no room for folios, which have to lie, like fallen warriors, on their sides.

All that is very true, particularly about housemaids.

14 January

My Books

Henry Wadsworth Longfellow (1807–1882)

Sadly as some old mediaeval knight
    Gazed at the arms he could no longer wield,
    The sword two-handed and the shining shield
    Suspended in the hall, and full in sight,
While secret longings for the lost delight
    Of tourney or adventure in the field
    Came over him, and tears but half concealed
    Trembled and fell upon his beard of white,
So I behold these books upon their shelf,
    My ornaments and arms of other days;
    Not wholly useless, though no longer used,
For they remind me of my other self,
    Younger and stronger, and the pleasant ways
    In which I walked, now clouded and confused.

The Princess and the Pea

From *Why Be Happy When You Could Be Normal?* 2011

Jeanette Winterson (1959–)

I used to work on the market on Saturdays, and after school on Thursdays and Fridays, packing up. I used the money to buy books. I smuggled them inside and hid them under the mattress.

Anybody with a single bed, standard size, and a collection of paperbacks, standard size, will know that seventy-two per layer can be accommodated under the mattress. By degrees my bed began to rise visibly like the Princess and the Pea, so that soon I was sleeping closer to the ceiling than the floor.

My mother was suspicious-minded, but even if she had not been, it was clear that her daughter was going up in the world.

One night she came in and saw the corner of a paperback sticking out from under the mattress. She pulled it out and examined it with her flashlight. It was an unlucky choice; D. H. Lawrence, *Women in Love.*

Mrs Winterson knew that Lawrence was a Satanist and a pornographer, and hurling it out of the window, she rummaged and rifled and I came tumbling off the bed while she threw book after book out of the window and into the backyard. I was grabbing books and trying to hide them, the dog was running off with them, my dad was standing helpless in his pyjamas.

When she had done, she picked up the little paraffin stove we used to heat the bathroom, went into the yard, poured paraffin over the books and set them on fire.

I watched them blaze and blaze and remember thinking how warm it was, how light, on the freezing Saturnian January night. And books have always been light and warmth to me.

Vulgar Behaviour

From *The School for Scandal, produced 1777*

Richard Sheridan (1751–1816)

Act I, scene i

Lady Sneerwell:
I wonder, Sir Benjamin, you never publish anything.

Sir Benjamin:
To say truth, ma'am, 'tis very vulgar to print. And as my little productions are mostly satires and lampoons on particular people, I find they circulate more by giving copies in confidence to the friends of the parties. However, I have some love elegies, which, when favoured with this lady's smiles, I mean to give the public.

Anyone Can Publish

From *The Diary of a Nobody, 1892* | George Grossmith (1847–1912) |
Weedon Grossmith (1854–1919)

Why should I not publish my diary? I have often seen reminiscences
of people I have never even heard of, and I fail to see – because
I do not happen to be a 'Somebody' why my diary should not be
interesting. My only regret is that I did not commence it when
I was a youth.

CHARLES POOTER.

The Laurels,
Brickfield Terrace,
Holloway.

Women and Fiction

From *A Room of One's Own, 1929* | Virginia Woolf (1882–1941)

The title women and fiction might mean, and you may have meant it to mean, women and what they are like; or it might mean women and the fiction that they write; or it might mean women and the fiction that is written about them; or it might mean that somehow all three are inextricably mixed together and you want me to consider them in that light. But when I began to consider the subject in this last way, which seemed the most interesting, I soon saw that it had one fatal drawback. I should never be able to come to a conclusion. I should never be able to fulfil what is, I understand, the first duty of a lecturer – to hand you after an hour's discourse a nugget of pure truth to wrap up between the pages of your notebooks and keep on the mantelpiece for ever. All I could do was to offer you an opinion upon one minor point – a woman must have money and a room of her own if she is to write fiction; and that, as you will see, leaves the great problem of the true nature of woman and the true nature of fiction unsolved. I have shirked the duty of coming to a conclusion upon these two questions – women and fiction remain, so far as I am concerned, unsolved problems.

Travels and Voyages

From *The Life of the Fields: Country Literature, 1884*

Richard Jefferies (1848–1887)

Every one when first exploring the world of books, and through them the larger world of reality, is attracted by travels and voyages. These are peculiarly interesting to country people, to whom the idea of exploration is natural. Reading such a book is like coming to a hill and seeing a fresh landscape spread out before them. There are no museums in the villages to familiarize them with the details of life in distant parts of the earth, so that every page as it is turned over brings something new. They understand the hardships of existence, hard food, exposure, the struggle with the storm, and can enter into the anxieties and privations of the earlier voyagers searching out the coast of America. They would rather read these than the most exciting novels.

20 January

On Homer

From *Of the Standard Taste, 1757* | David Hume (1711–1776)

The same HOMER who pleased at ATHENS and ROME two
thousand years ago, is still admired at PARIS and at LONDON.
All the changes of climate, government, religion, and language, have
not been able to obscure his glory. Authority or prejudice may give
a temporary vogue to a bad poet or orator, but his reputation will
never be durable or general. When his compositions are examined
by posterity or by foreigners, the enchantment is dissipated, and his
faults appear in their true colours. On the contrary, a real genius, the
longer his works endure, and the more wide they are spread, the more
sincere is the admiration which he meets with.

On First Looking into Chapman's Homer

John Keats (1795–1821)

Much have I travell'd in the realms of gold,
    And many goodly states and kingdoms seen;
    Round many western islands have I been
Which bards in fealty to Apollo hold.
Oft of one wide expanse had I been told
    That deep-brow'd Homer ruled as his demesne;
    Yet did I never breathe its pure serene
Till I heard Chapman speak out loud and bold:
Then felt I like some watcher of the skies
    When a new planet swims into his ken;
Or like stout Cortez when with eagle eyes
    He star'd at the Pacific – and all his men
Look'd at each other with a wild surmise –
    Silent, upon a peak in Darien.

The Life of a Book

From *The Gifts of Reading, 2016* | Robert Macfarlane (1976–)

During the solitary months and years spent writing a book, it can be easy to forget that it will – if you are lucky – live a social life: that your book might enter the imaginations and memories of its readers and thrive there, that your book might be crammed into pockets or backpacks and carried up mountains or to foreign countries, or that your book might be given by one person to another. Perhaps the aspect of authorship I cherish most are the glimpses I get of how my books are themselves carried, or are themselves given. When I sign books after readings, people frequently want their copies inscribed as gifts. *Would you make this out to my mother, who loves mountains? … to my brother, who lives in Calcutta? . . . to my best friend, who is ill? … to my father, who is no longer able to walk as far as he would wish?* Several times I've been asked to inscribe books to young children who can't yet read: *We want to give this book to them now, so it's waiting for them when they're ready for it.* These conversations with readers, and the stories that arise from them, are among the strongest forces that keep me writing.

The Perfect Position for a Bookshop

From *Riceyman Steps, 1923* | Arnold Bennett (1867–1931)

The shop was, in fact, well placed in Riceyman Steps. It had a picturesque air, and Riceyman Steps also had a picturesque air, with all its outworn shabbiness, grime and decay. The steps leading up to Riceyman Square, the glimpse of the Square at the top, with its church bearing a massive cross on the west front, the curious perpendicular effects of the tall, blind, ochreish houses – all these touched the imagination of every man who had in his composition any unusually strong admixture of the universal human passion – love of the past. The shop reinforced the appeal of its environment. The shop was in its right appropriate place. To the secret race of collectors always ravenously desiring to get something for much less than its real value, the window in Riceyman Steps was irresistible. And all manner of people, including book-collectors, passed along King's Cross Road in the course of a day. And all the collectors upon catching sight of the shop exclaimed in their hearts: 'What a queer spot for a bookshop! Bargains! …' Moreover, the business was of old date and therefore had firmly established connexions quite extra-local. Scores of knowing persons knew about it, and were proud of their knowledge. 'What!' they would say with affected surprise to acquaintances of their own tastes. 'You don't know Riceyman Steps, King's Cross Road? Best hunting-ground in London!' The name 'Riceyman' on a signboard, whose paint had been flaking off for twenty years, also enhanced the prestige of the shop, for it proved ancient local associations. Riceyman must be of the true ancient blood of Clerkenwell.

Letters to Susie Beever on Frondes Agrestes

From *Hortus Inclusus, 1887* | John Ruskin (1819–1900) |
Susie Beever (1805–1893)

Perugia, 12th June (1874)

I am more and more pleased at the thought of this gathering of
yours, and soon expect to tell you what the bookseller says.
Meantime I want you to think of the form the collection should take
with reference to my proposed re-publication. I mean to take the
botany, the geology, the Turner defence, and the general art criticism
of 'Modern Painters', as four separate books, cutting out nearly all
the preaching, and a good deal of the sentiment. Now what you find
pleasant and helpful to you of general maxim or reflection, must
be of some value; and I think therefore that your selection will just
do for me what no other reader could have done, least of all
I myself; keep together, that is to say, what may be right and true
of those youthful thoughts. I should like you to add anything that
specially pleases you, of whatever kind; but to keep the notion of
your book being the didactic one as opposed to the other picturesque
and scientific volumes, will I think help you in choosing between
passages when one or other is to be rejected.

Assisi, Sacristan's Cell, 25th June (1874)

This extract book of yours will be most precious in its help to me,
provided it is kept within somewhat narrow limits. As soon as it is
done I mean to have it published in a strong and pretty but *cheap*
form, and it must not be too bulky. Consider, therefore, not only
what you like, but how far and with whom each bit is likely to find
consent and service. You will have to choose perhaps, after a little
while, among what you have already chosen. I mean to leave it *wholly*
in your hands; it is to be Susie's choice of my writings.

Don't get into a flurry of responsibility, but don't at once write
down all you have a mind to; I know you'll find a good deal! for you
are exactly in sympathy with me in all things.

Lucca, 10th August (1874)

Now, Susie, invent a nice cluster of titles for the book and send them to me to choose from, to Hotel de l'Arno, Florence. I must get that out before the day of judgment, if I can. I'm so glad of your sweet flatteries in this note received to-day.

Florence, 25th August (1874)

I was a little scandalized at the idea of your calling the book 'word-painting'. My dearest Susie, it is the chief provocation of my life to be called a 'word-painter' instead of a thinker. I hope you haven't filled your book with descriptions. I thought it was the thoughts you were looking for?

'Posie' would be pretty. If you ask Joanie she will tell you perhaps *too* pretty for *me*.

Florence, 1st September (1874)

Don't be in despair about your book. I am sure it will be lovely. I'll see to it the moment I get home.

Wakefield, 25th January, 1875

Here's our book in form at last, and it seems to me just a nice size, and on the whole very taking. I've put a touch or two more to the preface, and I'm sadly afraid there's a naughty note somewhere. I hope you won't find it, and that you will like the order the things are put in.

Republishing

From *Frondes Agrestes: Readings in 'Modern Painters'
Chosen at her pleasure by the author's friend the younger
Lady of the Thwaite, Coniston, 1875*

John Ruskin (1819–1900) | Susie Beever (1805–1893)

Preface

I have been often asked to republish the first book of mine which
the public noticed, and which, hitherto, remains their favourite, in
a more easily attainable form than that of its existing editions. I am,
however, resolved never to republish the book as a whole; some parts
of it being, by the established fame of Turner, rendered unnecessary;
and others having been always useless, in their praise of excellence
which the public will never give the labour necessary to discern.
But, finding lately that one of my dearest friends, who, in advanced
age, retains the cheerfulness and easily delighted temper of bright
youth, had written out, for her own pleasure, a large number of
passages from 'Modern Painters' it seemed to me certain that what
such a person felt to be useful to herself, could not but be useful
also to a class of readers whom I much desired to please, and who
would sometimes enjoy, in my early writings, what I never should
myself have offered them. I asked my friend, therefore, to add to her
own already chosen series, any other passages she thought likely to
be of permanent interest to general readers; and I have printed her
selections in absolute submission to her judgment, merely arranging
the pieces she sent me in the order which seemed most convenient
for the reciprocal bearing of their fragmentary meanings, and adding
here and there an explanatory note; or, it may be, a deprecatory one,
in cases where my mind had changed.

Lists

Patrick Leigh Fermor (1915–2011)

[When Artemis Cooper was researching her biography of
Paddy Leigh Fermor in his house in Kardamyli, Greece,
she went through his files and came across the following.]

Detached Oddments
Not Very Important Oddments
Own Oddments
Own Unsorted Oddments
Unsorted but Interesting
Oldish – Needs Sorting
Badly Needs Sorting
Current: Unsorted
Current: Various
Vol III: Odds and Ends
Crete: Mixed Bag
Tiring Duplicates
Disjecta Membra
Scattered Intractables
Official Bumph
Flotsam

The Lumber Room

From *The Adventures of Sherlock Holmes:*
The Five Orange Pips, 1892 | Arthur Conan Doyle (1859–1930)

Sherlock Holmes: A man should keep his little brain attic stocked
with all the furniture that he is likely to use, and the rest he can
put away in the lumber room of his library, where he can get it
if he wants it.

A Selection of Awards and Prizes

Poet Laureate of the United Kingdom

The Poet Laureate is chosen by the monarch, with the advice of the government, and is an honorary post with no specific duties. Geoffrey Chaucer was given ten shillings a year by King Henry I, and in 1616 King James I of England granted a pension to Ben Jonson, but in 1668 King Charles II formally established the post of poet laureate and appointed John Dryden. Originally awarded for life, since 1999, the position has been awarded for a ten-year period.

The Nobel Prize for Literature

This was first awarded in 1901 and, like the other Nobel prizes, was created by Alfred Nobel in his will of 1895. The bulk of his assets formed a fund and each year the interest was to be awarded to those in five fields who 'have conferred the greatest benefit to humankind'. The Nobel Prize for Literature was to be awarded 'to the person who, in the field of literature, produced the most outstanding work in an idealistic direction'. The recipient is chosen by the Academy in Stockholm.

The Prix Goncourt

A French literary prize awarded each year to the author of an outstanding work of imaginative prose, usually a novel. Conceived in 1867 by the brothers Edmond and Jules de Goncourt and created in 1903, the winner is chosen by the Académie Goncourt, a literary society of ten members.

The Pulitzer Prize

The Pulitzer prizes and scholarships were founded by the inspirational nineteenth-century newspaper publisher Joseph Pulitzer. In letters, the original prizes were awarded to an American novel, play, work of history and biography, but the Plan of Award was intentionally flexible and there are now 21 awards.

The Booker Prize

Founded in 1969 and awarded by a panel of seven authors, librarians, literary agents, publishers and booksellers, the Booker Prize gives status and £50,000 to the winner. Since 2014 it has included any novel written in English.

Zora Neale Hurston

From *Their Eyes Were Watching God:*
What Does Soulful Mean? 2009 | Zadie Smith (1975–)

Above all, Hurston is essential universal reading because she is
neither self-conscious nor restricted. She was raised in the real
Eatonville, Florida, an all-black town; this unique experience went
some way to making Hurston the writer she was. She grew up a
fully human being, unaware that she was meant to consider herself
a minority, an other, an exotic or something depleted in rights,
talents, desires and expectations. As an adult, away from Eatonville,
she found the world was determined to do its best to remind her of
her supposed inferiority, but Hurston was already made, and the
metaphysical confidence she claimed for her life ('I am not tragically
colored') is present, with equal, refreshing force, in her fiction. She
liked to yell 'Culllaaaah Struck!' when she entered a fancy party –
almost everybody was. But Hurston herself was not. 'Blackness', as
she understood it and wrote about it, is as natural and inevitable
and complete to her as, say, 'Frenchness' is to Flaubert. It is also as
complicated, as full of blessings and curses. One can be no more
removed from it than from one's arm, but it is no more the total
measure of one's being than an arm is.

John Aubrey: Odds and Ends

From *A Literary Pilgrim in England, 1917*

Edward Thomas (1878–1917)

John Aubrey was a gossip whose odds and ends about men, things, and places, are now better than most full-dress literature. Those about men were set down at first merely as material for a biographer whom he thought his better, Anthony à Wood, and, as he was inquisitive and precise, there were some strange things amongst them, so that he said they were 'not fit to let fly abroad till about thirty years hence, for the author and the persons (like medlars) ought to be first rotten.' They were 'put in writing tumultuarily,' and he fancied himself 'all along discoursing' with Wood. The *Brief Lives* will now survive whatever is made out of them. So with his observations of antiquities and natural history. Who but Aubrey would have noticed and entered in a book that in the spring after the Fire of London 'all the ruins were overgrown with an herb or two, but especially with a yellow flower, *Ericolevis Neapolitana*'?

FEBRUARY

Frivolous and Idle Books

The Perfect Bookshop

From *The Unknown Unknown, 2014* | Mark Forsyth (1977–)

It doesn't matter what the book is. It's the one that caught your eye. Or perhaps it's just the one that caught your hand. But in a Good Bookshop that is good enough. In a Good Bookshop all the books are good.

Half the art of bookselling is about choosing what *not* to have in your shop. It is not enough to have good books, you must not have bad books.

If a bookshop contained every book ever written, what are the chances that you would find the one book you need? Well, they'd be perfect if you *already knew* what you needed, but, as I have been saying, that is not the point of a bookshop. That's something for the internet. No, the perfect bookshop is small, small and selective.

You should be able to go in blindfolded, reach out your hand at random and find something wonderful. I mean, I'm not actually recommending you go into a bookshop blindfolded and try this. You'd probably knock something over. Or accidentally punch a bookseller in the face. But you see the principle? Small and perfectly stocked.

Serendipity in Hatchards Bookshop

Jane McMorland Hunter (1960–)

As well as editing and writing books, I work in Hatchards Bookshop in Piccadilly, London. I started there as a Christmas temp in 1982 and misunderstood the word 'temp'. I'm still there. Obviously I think it's a Good Bookshop, in fact I think it's the best. And, I think, what follows proves my point.

I usually work on the second floor (children's and cookery) but one busy day I had to go down to the first floor (fiction, poetry, literary criticism, etc.) to find a book for a customer. I swept past the desk and my elbow sent a display of little books flying. As I picked them up, put them back and straightened the pile, I noticed the title: *The Unknown Unknown* by Mark Forsyth. My curiosity was aroused and, as well as the book for the customer, I took a copy of this little book back up to the second floor. I read it and loved it, not least because the way I had found it suited the book. I had had no idea that it existed before chance, or serendipity, brought it into contact with my elbow.

To quote Donald Rumsfeld in Mark Forsyth's book:

'There are things we know that we know. There are known unknowns. That is to say there are things that we know we don't know. But there are also unknown unknowns. There are things we do not know we don't know.'

As *The Unknown Unknown* shows, this statement, which might appear perplexing but doesn't, if you think about it, applies perfectly to books.

Pronunciation Dictionaries

From *The Life of Samuel Johnson, 1791* | James Boswell (1740–1795)

Boswell: 'It may be of use, Sir, to have a Dictionary to ascertain the pronunciation.'

Johnson: 'Why, Sir, my Dictionary shows you the accent of words, if you can but remember them.'

Boswell: 'But, Sir, we want marks to ascertain the pronunciation of the vowels. Sheridan, I believe, has finished such a work.'

Johnson: 'Why, Sir, consider how much easier it is to learn a language by the ear, than by any marks. Sheridan's Dictionary may do very well; but you cannot always carry it about with you: and, when you do want the word, you have not the Dictionary. It is like a man who has a sword that will not draw. It is an admirable sword, to be sure: but while your enemy is cutting your throat, you are unable to use it. Besides, Sir, what entitles Sheridan to fix the pronunciation of English? He has, in the first place, the disadvantage of being an Irishman: and if he says he will fix it after the example of the best company, why they differ among themselves. I remember an instance: when I published the Plan for my Dictionary, Lord Chesterfield told me that the word *great* should be pronounced so as to rhyme to *state*; and Sir William Yonge sent me word that it should be pronounced so as to rhyme to seat, and that none but an Irishman would pronounce it *grait*. Now here were two men of the highest rank, the one, the best speaker in the House of Lords, the other, the best speaker in the House of Commons, differing entirely.'

Good Books

From *Areopagitica: A speech of Mr. John Milton for the Liberty of Unlicenced Printing, to the Parliament of England, 1644* |

John Milton (1608–1674)

Books are not absolutely dead things, but do contain a potency of life in them to be as active as that soul was whose progeny they are; nay they do preserve as in a vial the purest efficacy and extraction of that living intellect that bread them. I know they are as lively, and as vigorously productive, as those fabulous dragon's teeth; and being sown up and down, may chance to spring up armed men. And yet on the other hand, unless wariness be used, as good almost kill a man as kill a good book: who kills a man kills a reasonable creature, God's image; but he who destroys a good book, kills reason itself, kills the image of God, as it were in the eye. Many a man lives a burden to the Earth; but a good book is the precious life-blood a master spirit, embalmed and treasured up on purpose to a life beyond life. 'Tis true, no age can restore a life, whereof perhaps there is no great loss; and revolutions of ages do not oft recover the loss of a rejected truth, for the want of which whole nations fare the worse.

Saving Time

From *Letters to His Son on the Art of Becoming a Man of the World and a Gentleman, published 1774*

Lord Chesterfield (1694–1773)

Letter CLXXXIV
London, Feb. the 5th, O. S. 1750

Many people lose a great deal of time by reading: for they read frivolous and idle books; such as the absurd Romances of the last two centuries; where characters, that never existed, are insipidly displayed, and sentiments, that were never felt, pompously described: the oriental ravings and extravagances of the Arabian Nights, and Mogul Tales: or, the new flimsy brochures that now swarm in France, of Fairy Tales, *Réflexions sur le Cœur at l'Esprit, Métaphysique de l'Amour, Analyse des beaux Sentiments;* and such sort of idle frivolous stuff, that nourishes and improves the mind just as much as whipped cream would the body. Stick to the best established books in every language; the celebrated Poets, Historians, Orators or Philosophers. By these means (to use a city metaphor) you will make fifty per cent. of that time, of which others do not make above three or four, or probably nothing at all.

5 February

Causality

From *A Swim in a Pond in the Rain*, 2021

George Saunders (1958–)

I've worked with so many wildly talented young writers over the years that I feel qualified to say that there are two things that separate writers who go on to publish from those who don't.

First, a willingness to revise.

Second the extent to which the writer has learned to make causality.

Making causality doesn't seem sexy or particularly literary. It's a workmanlike thing, to make A cause B, the stuff of vaudeville, of Hollywood. But it's the hardest thing to learn. It doesn't come naturally, not to most of us. But that's really all a story is: a series of things that happen in sequence, in which we can discern a pattern of causality.

. . . .

Causality is to the writer what melody is to the songwriter: a super-power that the audience feels as the crux of the matter; the thing the audience actually shows up for; the hardest thing to do; that which distinguishes the competent practitioner from the extraordinary one.

A well-written bit of prose is like a beautifully hand-painted kite, lying there on the grass. It's nice. We admire it. Causality is the wind that comes along and lifts it up. The kite is then a beautiful thing made even more beautiful by the fact that it's doing what it was made to do.

Puck

From *Diary, 1870, 1871* | Francis Kilvert (1840–1879)

Friday 28th October

Hot coppers, too much wine last night and an ill temper this morning. Reading Puck by 'Ouida', a book Morrell lent me. The authoress seems to have a rabid hatred of women and parsons.

Tuesday 7th February

Finished reading Puck, clever, bitter, extravagant, full of repetitions and absurdities and ludicrous ambitious attempts at fine writing, weak and bombastic. The great blot is the insane and vicious hatred of women. Evidently written by a woman.

An Idle Rogueish Book

From *Diary* | Samuel Pepys (1633–1703)

Feb. 8, 1668

Thence away to the Strand, to my bookseller's, and there staid an hour, and bought the idle, rogueish book, *L'escholle des filles*, which I have bought in plain binding, avoiding the buying of it better bound, because I resolve, as soon as I have read it, to burn it, that it may not stand in the list of books, nor among them, to disgrace them if it should be found. Thence home, and busy late at the office, and then home to supper and to bed.

To Be Seen to Be Reading

From *The Complete Polysyllabic Spree, 2006* | Nick Hornby (1957–)

February 2006

If, as a recent survey in the UK suggested, most people buy books because they like to be *seen* reading rather than because they actually enjoy it, then I would suggest that you can't beat a collection of letters by an author – and if that author is a poet, then so much the better. The implication is clear: you know the poet's work inside out (indeed, what you're saying is that if you read his or her entire oeuvre one more time, then the lines would ring round and round in your head like a Kelly Clarkson tune), and you now need something else, something that might help to shed some light on some of the more obscure couplets.

9 February

The Importance of Dictionaries

From *The Private Library, 1897* | A. L. Humphreys (1865–1946)

Junior Assistant and later Partner, Hatchards Bookshop (1881–1924)

Let us not be afraid of using a dictionary. *A* dictionary? A dozen; at all events, until Dr Murray's huge undertaking is finished. And even then, for no one dictionary will help us through some authors – say, Chaucer, or Spenser, or Sir Thomas Browne. Let us use our full lexicon, and Latin dictionary, and French dictionary, and Anglo-Saxon dictionary, and etymological dictionary, and dictionaries of antiquity, and biography, and geography, and concordances, anything and everything that will throw light on the meanings and histories of words.

Blackwood's Magazine, February, 1896.

Definitions and Remarks

From *Dictionary of Phrase and Fable, 1895*

Rev. Ebenezer Cobham Brewer (1810–1897)

Book. (Ang-Saxon, *boc;* Danish, *beuke,* German, *buche,* a beech-tree). Beech-bark was employed for carving names on before the invention of printing.

> Here on my trunk's surviving frame
> Carved many a long-forgotten name …
> As love's own alter, honour me:
> Spare, woodman, spare the beechen tree.
>
> *Campbell: The Beech Tree's Petition*

Book. *The dearest ever sold.* A Mazarin Bible at the Thorold sale, in 1884, bought by Mr Quaritch, bookseller, Piccadilly, London, for £3,900. In 1873 Lord Ashburnham gave £3,400 for a copy.

Book. *The oldest in the world.* That by Ptah-Hotep, the Egyptian, complied in the reign of Assa, about B.C. 3366. This MS. Is preserved in the Bibliothèque Nationale in Paris. It is written on papyrus in hieratic characters, and is a compilation of moral, political and religious aphorisms. It strongly insists on reverence to women, politeness and monotheism.

Book-keeper. One who borrows books, but does not return them.

Bookworm. One always poring over his books: so called in allusion to the insect that eats holes in books, and lives both in and on its leaves.

Library. One of the most approved materials for writing on, before the invention of paper, was the thin rind between the solid wood and the outside bark of certain trees. This substance is called in Latin *liber,* which came in time to signify also a 'book'. Hence our library, the place for books; *librarian,* the keeper of books; and the French *livre,* a book.

Definitions

From *A Dictionary of the English Language, 1755*

Samuel Johnson (1709–1784)

Dull. To make dictionaries is dull work.

Lexicographer. A writer of dictionaries, a harmless drudge.

Patron. Commonly a wretch who supports with insolence, and is paid with flattery.

'Our Library is Not Like Others'

From *The Name of the Rose, 1980* | Umberto Eco (1932–2016)

Translated by William Weaver (1923–2013)

[The abbot:] 'As long as these walls stand, we shall be the custodians of the divine Word.'

'Amen,' William said in a devout tone. 'But what has this to do with the fact that the library may not be visited?'

'You see, Brother William,' the abbot said, 'to achieve the immense and holy task that enriches these walls' – and he nodded toward the bulk of the Aedificium, which could be glimpsed from the cell's windows, towering above the abbatial church itself – 'devout men have toiled for centuries, observing iron rules. The library was laid out on a plan which has remained obscure to all over the centuries, and which none of the monks is called upon to know. Only the librarian has received the secret, from the librarian who preceded him, and he communicates it, while still alive, to the assistant librarian, so that death will not take him by surprise and rob the community of the knowledge. And the secret seals the lips of both men. Only the librarian has, in addition to that knowledge, the right to move through the labyrinth of the books, he alone knows where to find them and where to replace them, he alone is responsible for their safekeeping. The other monks work in the scriptorium and may know the list of the volumes that the library houses. But a list of titles often tells very little; only the librarian knows, from the collocation of the volume, from its degrees of inaccessibility, what secrets, what truths or falsehoods, the volume contains. Only he decides how, when, and whether to give it to the monk who requests it; sometimes he first consults me. Because not all truths are for all ears, not all falsehoods can be recognized as such by a pious soul; and the monks, finally, are in the scriptorium to carry out a precise task, which requires them to read certain volumes and not others, and not to pursue every foolish curiosity that seizes them, whether through weakness of intellect or through pride or through diabolical prompting.'

Tyndale's Ploughman's Translation

From *Tyndale's New Testament, 1534* | William Tyndale (c. 1494–1536)

[Translated so 'a boy that driveth the plough to know more scripture than the clergy of the day'.]

The Fyrst Pistle of Paul the Apostle to the Corrynthyans, chapter XIII

Though I speake with the tonges of men and angels and yet had no love I were even as soundinge brasse: and as a tynklynge Cymball. And though I coulde prophesy and understode all secretes and all knowledge: yee if I had all fayth so that I coulde move moutayns (oute of ther places) and yet had no love I were nothynge. And though I bestowed all my gooddes to fede the poore and though I gave my body even that I burned and yet had no love it profeteth me nothynge.

Love suffreth longe, and is corteous. Love envieth nott. Love doth nott frawardly swelleth not, dealeth not dishonestly, seketh nott her awne, is not provoked to anger, thynketh not evyll reioyseth not in iniquite: but reioyseth in the trueth, suffreth all thynge, beleveth all thynges hopeth all thynges, endureth in all thynges. Though that prophesyinge fayle, other tonges shall cease, or knowledge vanysshe awaye: yet love falleth never awaye.

For oure knowledge is unparfet, and oure prophesyinge is unperfet: but when that which is parfet is come: then that which is unparfet shall be done awaye. When I was a chylde, I spake as a chylde, I understode as a childe, I ymagened as a chylde: but as sone as I was a man I put awaye childesshnes. Now we se in a glasse even in a darke speakynge: but then shall we se face to face. Now I knowe unparfectly: but then shall I knowe even as I am knowen. Nowe abideth faith, hope, and love, even these thre: but the chefe of these is love.

The English Bible

From *Essay on Dryden, Edinburgh Review, 1828*

Thomas Babington Macaulay (1800–1859)

The English Bible, a book which, if everything else in our language should perish, would alone suffice to show the whole extent of its beauty and power. The respect which the translators felt for the original prevented them from adding any of the hideous decorations then in fashion. The ground-work of the version, indeed, was of an earlier age. The familiarity with which the Puritans, on almost every occasion, used the Scriptural phrases was no doubt very ridiculous; but it produced good effects. It was a cant; but it drove out a cant far more offensive.

An Apology for the Devil

From *Note-books, 1912* | Samuel Butler (1835–1902)

It must be remembered that we have only heard one side of the case.
God has written all the books.

The Appeal of Reading

From *The Uncommon Reader, 2006* | Alan Bennett (1934–)

[Having discovered the City of Westminster travelling library by chance, the Queen becomes an avid reader.]

The appeal of reading, she thought, lay in its indifference: there was something lofty about literature. Books did not care who was reading them or whether one read them or not. All readers were equal, herself included. Literature, she thought, is a commonwealth; letters a republic. Actually she had heard this phrase, the republic of letters, used before, at graduation ceremonies, honorary degrees and the like, though without knowing what it meant. At that time talk of a republic of any sort she had thought mildly insulting and in her actual presence tactless to say the least. It was only now she understood what it meant. Books did not defer. All readers were equal, and this took her back to the beginning of her life. As a girl, one of her greatest thrills had been on VE night, when she and her sister had slipped out of the gates and mingled unrecognised with the crowds. There was something of that, she felt, to reading. It was anonymous; it was shared; it was common. And she who led a life apart now found she craved it. Here in these pages and between these covers she could go unrecognised.

The Library at Westminster Abbey

From *Sketch Book: The Mutability of Literature, 1819–1820*
Washington Irving (1783–1859)

I had taken down a thick little quarto, curiously bound in
parchment, with brass clasps, and seated myself at a table in
a venerable elbow-chair. Instead of reading, however, I was
beguiled by the solemn monastic air, and the lifeless quiet of the
place, into a train of musing.

. . . .

While I sat half-murmuring, half-meditating, these unprofitable
speculations with my head resting on my hand, I was thrumming
with the other hand upon the quarto, until I accidentally loosened
the clasps; when, to my utter astonishment, the little book gave two
or three yawns, like one awaking from a deep sleep, then a husky
hem; and at length began to talk. At first its voice was very hoarse
and broken, being much troubled by a cobweb which some studious
spider had woven across it, and having probably contracted a cold
from long exposure to the chills and damps of the abbey. In a short
time, however, it became more distinct, and I soon found it an
exceedingly fluent, conversable little tome. Its language, to be sure,
was rather quaint and obsolete, and its pronunciation what, in the
present day, would be deemed barbarous; but I shall endeavor, as far
as I am able, to render it in modern parlance.

It began with railings about the neglect of the world – about merit
being suffered to languish in obscurity, and other such commonplace
topics of literary repining, and complained bitterly that it had not
been opened for more than two centuries. That the dean only looked
now and then into the library, sometimes took down a volume or
two, trifled with them for a few moments, and then returned them
to their shelves. 'What a plague do they mean?' said the little quarto,
which I began to perceive was somewhat choleric, 'what a plague do
they mean by keeping several thousand volumes of us shut up here,
and watched by a set of old vergers, like so many beauties in a harem,

merely to be looked at now and then by the dean? Books were written to give pleasure and to be enjoyed; and I would have a rule passed that the dean should pay each of us a visit at least once a year; or, if he is not equal to the task, let them once in a while turn loose the whole school of Westminster among us, that at any rate we may now and then have an airing.'

'Softly, my worthy friend,' replied I; 'you are not aware how much better you are off than most books of your generation. By being stored away in this ancient library you are like the treasured remains of those saints and monarchs which lie enshrined in the adjoining chapels, while the remains of their contemporary mortals, left to the ordinary course of Nature, have long since returned to dust.'

'Sir,' said the little tome, ruffling his leaves and looking big, 'I was written for all the world, not for the bookworms of an abbey. I was intended to circulate from hand to hand, like other great contemporary works; but here have I been clasped up for more than two centuries, and might have silently fallen a prey to these worms that are playing the very vengeance with my intestines if you had not by chance given me an opportunity of uttering a few last words before I go to pieces.'

Good Poetry

From *Gossip in a Library, 1891* | Edmund Gosse (1849–1928)

Good poetry seems to be almost as indestructible as diamonds. You throw it out of window into the roar of London, it disappears in a deep brown slush, the omnibus and the growler pass over it, and by and by it turns up again somewhere uninjured, with all the pure fire lambent in its facets. No doubt thoroughly good specimens of prose do get lost, dragged down the vortex of a change of fashion, and never thrown back again to light. But the quantity of excellent verse produced in any generation is not merely limited, but keeps very fairly within the same proportions. The verse-market is never really glutted, and while popular masses of what Mr Browning calls 'deciduous trash' survive their own generation, only to be carted away, the little excellent, unnoticed book gradually pushes its path up silently into fame.

On His Books

Hilaire Belloc (1870–1953)

When I am dead, I hope it may be said:
'His sins were scarlet, but his books were read.'

Three Poets

From *On Poetry: A Rhapsody, 1733,*

Jonathan Swift (1667–1745)

Lines 1–24

All Human Race would fain be *Wits,*
And Millions miss, for one that hits.
Young's universal Passion, *Pride,*
Was never known to spread so wide.
Say, *Britain,* cou'd you ever boast, –
Three Poets in an Age at most?
Our chilling Climate hardly bears
A *Sprig* of Bays in Fifty Years;
While every Fool his Claim alleges,
As if it grew in common Hedges.
What Reason can there be assign'd
For this Perverseness in the Mind?
Brutes find out where their Talents lie:
A *Bear* will not attempt to fly:
A founder'd *Horse* will oft debate,
Before he tries a five-barr'd Gate;
A *Dog* by Instinct turns aside,
Who sees the Ditch too deep and wide.
But *Man* we find the only Creature
Who, led by *Folly,* fights with *Nature*;
Who, when *she* loudly cries, *Forbear,*
With Obstinacy fixes there;
And, where his *Genius* least inclines,
Absurdly bends his whole Designs.

Saying it With Clay

From *My Name is Book: An Autobiography, 2014*

John Agard (1949–)

I like to think of clay tablets as my ancestors. Yes, I'll have you know that fired earth is part of Book's family tree, for clay tablets weren't just used to keep business records, lists and accounts. On clay tablets the Sumerians also stored secrets about the stars, as well as prayers, hymns and poets, and what's said to be the oldest story ever written down.

And what did they use for a pen? A reed. This ancient way of writing is called cuneiform, which means 'wedge-shaped', because they used a reed stylus with a wedge-shaped tip to press into the soft clay.

Sounds like hard work. You try writing on squishy lumps of clay. Then you've got to sun-dry the clay or bake it in a fire, and if it cracks, well, there goes your paper. But, of course, the Sumerians weren't short of clay for they lived on the banks of two great rivers.

Here on the shelf, centuries later, I often wonder what it would feel like to be a clay tablet stored in a jar with a poem or story inscribed on me, and then to be dug up thousands of years later by an archaeologist searching among ruins in some faraway desert. Yes, I enjoy a bit of daydreaming – don't we all?

Then I look around at my friends, paperbacks and hardbacks, all of us huddled together on the shelves and I say to myself, What's got into you, Book? Your paper pages would go all brown and crunchy in the heat of the desert.

Codex versus Scroll

From *The Secret Life of Books, 2019* | Tom Mole (1976–)

The codex form emerged long before print, in the first centuries of
the Common Era. It consists of a series of leaves stacked on top of
one another and gathered together along one edge. In other words,
it's the book as we know it. The book in your hands – if you're
reading a paper version rather than the e-book – is a codex, just
like, (I'm fairly sure) more or less all the paper books you will
have encountered.

Early readers of the codex praised it for being portable and easy to
handle compared with the scroll. It allows a reader to flick through
the pages and dip in and out, in a way that isn't so easy to do with
a scroll that has to be unrolled and rolled up again. Despite these
advantages, however, the codex took a long time to catch on. The
evidence of surviving books suggests that it slowly gained ground
over the scroll between about 100 and 500 CE. It's not a coincidence
that these were the years when Christianity was also gaining
converts. Christians were early adopters of the codex. They helped to
refine the techniques required to make codices (the plural of codex),
and they particularly favoured the codex form for their scriptures.
As Christianity became widespread, so the Christians' preferred form
of the book also took off.

Books versus Parchment

From *On Books and the Housing of Them, 1890*

W. E. Gladstone (1809–1898)

The form of the book, however, has gone through many variations; and we moderns have a great advantage in the shape which the exterior has now taken. It speaks to us symbolically by the title on its back, as the roll of parchment could hardly do.

Electronic Replicas versus Old Fashioned Books

From *The British Library and the St Pancras Building, 1994*

Sir Anthony Kenny (1931–)

Given the rapid obsolescence of information technology, the
electronic replicas once made would constantly need costly
retranscription. Otherwise superannuated platforms would have to be
specially maintained by computer antiquarians in order to make sure
that the texts remained accessible. Old fashioned books may fade and
decay; but the technology for human access to their contents, so long
as they survive, has not changed since the invention of spectacles.

25 February

How to Please an Author

From *Pudd'nhead Wilson, 1894* | Mark Twain (1835–1910)

There are three infallible ways of pleasing an author, and the three form a rising scale of compliment: 1, to tell him you have read one of his books; 2, to tell him you have read all of his books; 3, to ask him to let you read the manuscript of his forthcoming book. No. 1 admits you to his respect; No. 2 admits you to his admiration; No. 3 carries you clear into his heart. *Pudd'nhead Wilson's Calendar.*

Publishing and Books

From English Bards and Scotch Reviewers

Lord George Gordon Byron (1788–1824)

Prepare for rhyme – I'll publish, right or wrong:
Fools are my theme, let satire be my song.

. . . .

'Tis pleasant, sure, to see one's name in print;
A Book's a Book, altho' there's nothing in't.

The Meaning of Fiction

From *The Importance of Being Earnest, 1895*

Oscar Wilde (1854–1900)

MISS PRISM: You must put away your diary, Cecily. I really don't see why you should keep a diary at all.

CECILY: I keep a diary in order to enter the wonderful secrets of my life. If I didn't write them down I should probably forget all about them.

MISS PRISM: Memory, my dear Cecily, is the diary that we all carry about with us.

CECILY: Yes, but it usually chronicles the things that have never happened, and couldn't possibly have happened. I believe that Memory is responsible for nearly all the three-volume novels that Mudie sends us.

MISS PRISM: Do not speak slightingly of the three-volume novel, Cecily. I wrote one myself in earlier days.

CECILY: Did you really Miss Prism? How wonderfully clever you are! I hope it did not end happily? I don't like novels that end happily. They depress me so much.

MISS PRISM: The good ended happily, and the bad unhappily. That is what Fiction means.

CECILY: I suppose so. But it seems very unfair. And was your novel ever published?

MISS PRISM: Alas! no. The manuscript unfortunately was abandoned. I use the word in the sense of lost or mislaid. To your work child. These speculations are profitless.

28 February

Little Reading

From *Walden; or, Life in the Woods, 1854*

Henry David Thoreau (1817–1862)

There is a work in several volumes in our Circulating Library entitled *Little Reading*, which I thought referred to a town of that name which I had not been to.

MARCH

A Stroke of the Pen

The Author's Object

From *The Pickwick Papers: Preface, 1837*
Charles Dickens (1812–1870)

The author's object in this work, was to place before the reader a
constant succession of characters and incidents; to paint them in
as vivid colours as he could command; and to render them, at the
same time life-like and amusing.

Deferring to the judgment of others in the outset of the
undertaking, he adopted the machinery of the club, which was
suggested as that best adapted to his purpose: but, finding that it
tended rather to his embarrassment than otherwise, he gradually
abandoned it, considering it a matter of very little importance to the
work whether strictly epic justice were awarded to the club, or not.

The publication of the book in monthly numbers, containing
only thirty-two pages in each, rendered it an object of paramount
importance that while the different incidents were linked together
by a chain of interest strong enough to prevent their appearing
unconnected or impossible, the general design should be so simple
as to sustain no injury from this detached and desultory form of
publication, extending over no fewer than twenty months. In short,
it was necessary – or it appeared so to the author – that every number
should be, to a certain extent, complete in itself, and yet that the
whole twenty numbers, when collected, should form one tolerably
harmonious whole, each leading to the other by a gentle and not
unnatural progress of adventure.

The Success of *The Pickwick Papers*

From *Great English Novelists, 1908*

George Holbrook Jackson (1874–1948)

Pickwick was not an instantaneous success, and at one point the publishers were so disheartened that they were ready to throw up the venture. But just when their faith in the thing was at its lowest, Sam Weller appeared, and the *Pickwick Papers* burst into sudden and immense popularity. Only four hundred copies of the first part were ordered from the binders, but with Part XV the order had risen to forty thousand. Charles Dickens, at the age of twenty-four, became in a few weeks the most talked-about writer of the day, and *Pickwick* the most widely read book. He had sounded a new note in literature, and with a stroke of the pen almost made a new era for the novel. He did even more than this, he made fiction a thoroughly democratic and popular art, without degrading it. His robust humour and genial satire found their way to all hearts, and the vivid creatures of his fancy at once took up their places as common objects of the imagination of the whole nation. Everybody read and everybody enjoyed *Pickwick*.

The price Messrs. Chapman and Hall originally agreed to pay Dickens for the *Pickwick Papers* was £14 per month; this sum was afterwards increased to £15, but as the success of the venture increased further cheques were sent to him, and when the monthly instalments had finished he had made out of it between two thousand five hundred and three thousand pounds. This Dickens considered inadequate payment, and in the light of the fact that the publishers made something like twenty thousand pounds out of the book, a book by the way which they were at one time on the point of abandoning, the proportion of payment does not strike one as altogether fair. However, Dickens won something of more value than mere money: he won the hearts of the people, and from henceforth the world of letters was his and he could dictate his terms.

The New Contract

From *Vile Bodies, 1930* | Evelyn Waugh (1903–1966)

[Adam tells his publisher that the manuscript of his memoirs has been burnt by customs officials. Sam Benfleet does 'his best'.]

There was a longish pause while Sam Benfleet thought.

'What worries me is how are we going to make that sound convincing to old Rampole.'

'I should think it sounded convincing enough.'

'You don't know old Rampole. It's sometimes very difficult for me, Adam, working under him. Now if I had my own way I'd say, "Take your own time. Start again. Don't worry." But there's old Rampole. He's a devil for contracts, you know, and you did *say*, didn't you … ? It's all very difficult. You know, I wish it hadn't happened.'

'So do I, oddly enough,' said Adam.

'There's another difficulty. You've had an advance already, haven't you? Fifty pounds, wasn't it? Well, you know, *that* makes things very difficult. Old Rampole never likes big advances like that to young authors. You know I hate to say it, but I can't help feeling that the best thing would be for you to repay the advance – plus interest, of course, old Rampole would insist on that – and cancel the contract. Then if you ever thought of rewriting the book, well, of course, we should be delighted to consider it. I suppose that – well, I mean, it *would* be quite *convenient*, and all that, to repay the advance?'

'Not only inconvenient, but impossible,' said Adam in no particular manner.

There was another pause.

'Deuced awkward,' said Sam Benfleet 'It's a shame the way the Customs House officers are allowed to take the law into their own hands. Quite ignorant men, too. Liberty of the subject, I mean, and all that. I tell you what we'll do. We'll start a correspondence about it in the *New Statesman* … It is all so deuced awkward. But I think I can see a way out. I suppose you could get the book rewritten in

82

time for the Spring List? Well, we'll cancel the contract and forget all about the advance. No, no, my dear fellow, don't thank me. If only I was alone here I'd be doing that kind of thing all day. Now instead we'll have a new contract. It won't be quite so good as the last, I'm afraid. Old Rampole wouldn't stand for that. I'll tell you what, we'll give you our standard first-novel contract. I've got a printed form here. It won't take a minute to fill up. Just sign here.'

'May I just see the terms?'

'Of course, my dear fellow. They look a bit hard at first, I know, but it's our usual form. We made a very special case for you, you know. It's very simple. No royalty on the first two thousand, then a royalty of two and a half per cent., rising to five per cent. on the tenth thousand. We retain serial, cinema, dramatic, American, Colonial and translation rights, of course. And, of course, an option on your next twelve books on the same terms. It's a very straightforward arrangement really. Doesn't leave room for any of the disputes which embitter the relations of author and publisher. Most of our authors are working on a contract like that ... Splendid. Now don't you bother any more about that advance. I understand *perfectly*, and I'll square old Rampole somehow, even if it comes out of my director's fees.'

'Square old Rampole,' repeated Mr Benfleet thoughtfully as Adam went downstairs It was fortunate, he reflected, that none of the authors ever came across the senior partner, that benign old gentleman, who once a week drove up to board meetings from the country, whose chief interest in the business was confined to the progress of a little book of his own about bee-keeping, which they had published twenty years ago and, though he did not know it, allowed long ago to drop out of print. He often wondered in his uneasy moments what he would find to say when Rampole died.

Prose and Poetry: Lines

Jeremy Bentham (1748–1832)

Prose is when all the lines except the last go to the end. Poetry is when some of them fall short of it.

Prose and Poetry: Words

Samuel Taylor Coleridge (1772–1834)

I wish our clever young poets would remember my homely
definitions of prose and poetry; that is, prose = words in their
best order;– poetry = the best words in the best order.

Poetry Was Different

From *Cloud Busting (a story told in verse)*, 2004

Malorie Blackman (1962–)

A Note from the Author

I started writing poems for my own amusement long before I began
to write stories. Nursery rhymes, playground songs and pop songs
were as much a part of my life as breathing. I was reading at an early
age, but this was a deliberate, though fun, activity. Reading was
something I had to be taught, something I had to sit down and do.
Poetry was different. Poetry for me was in the way the branches of a
tree danced in the wind, in the way snow fell to the ground bringing
silence with it, in running water, in smiles, in music, in skipping
songs, in insults, in chants – poetry was everywhere.

The Books in Looking-Glass House

From *Through the Looking-Glass, and What Alice Found There, 1871, post-dated 1872* | Lewis Carroll (1832–1898)

First, there's the room you can see through the glass – that's just the same as our drawing-room, only the things go the other way. I can see all of it when I get upon a chair – all but a bit just behind the fireplace. Oh! I do so wish I could see *that* bit! I want so much to know whether they've a fire in the winter: you never can tell, you know, unless our fire smokes, and then smoke comes up in that room too – but that may be only pretence, just to make it look as if they had a fire. Well then, the books are something like our books, only the words go the wrong way: I know *that*, because I've held up one of our books to the glass, and then they hold up one in the other room.

7 March

Writing Books

From *Unpacking My Library, 1931* | Walter Benjamin (1892–1940)

Of all the ways of acquiring books, writing them oneself is regarded as the most praiseworthy method.

. . . .

Writers are really people who write books not because they are poor, but they are dissatisfied with the books which they could buy but do not like. You, ladies and gentlemen, may regard this as a whimsical definition of a writer. But everything said from the angle of a real collector is whimsical.

8 March

Lara

From *Manifesto, 2021* | Bernardine Evaristo (1959–)

I first *drafted* the book in prose, even though I'd never written prose
fiction and struggled to believe myself capable of the task in hand.
This didn't stop me, because the urge to write my parents' story was
so insistent. After three years, I had an unfinished manuscript of
two hundred pages written on an electronic typewriter, but it was
all over the place – a right mess. I had no understanding of narrative
structure, and the spirit of poetry that had infused and energized my
writing up to this point had disappeared. In making the transition
from poetry to prose, my use of language fell into a coma. Painfully,
I admitted to myself that, as I derived no pleasure from reading back
what I'd written, neither would anyone else. I still wanted to tell this
story, but I had no idea how to do it.

Three years in, I attended an Arvon Foundation residential writers'
course in the countryside, with no plans to go to any classes but to
sneakily use it as a writing retreat. The organizers weren't having
this, so I was made to show up for workshops, and in one session
I found myself writing a poem for an exercise, my first poem in over
three years, and I instantly reconnected to my love of language.
I knew then what I had to do. When I returned to London, I threw
the original manuscript of Lara into the bin, literally, so that it
disappeared without trace, and embarked on rewriting the story as
poetry. Discarding the manuscript was a necessary symbolic gesture
for me in order to start completely afresh, although I wish I hadn't.
I like to keep records of everything I write.

9 March

. . . .

I never regretted spending three years producing a discarded first
version of the book, because that's not how I saw it – then or with
future work. The creative process for me is an experiment – trial and
error – a trip into the unknown, which leads to new discoveries.

Dealer in Words

From *Sword Blades and Poppy Seeds, 1914* | Amy Lowell (1874–1925)

He took a shagreen letter case
From his pocket, and with charming grace
Offered me a printed card.
I read the legend, "Ephraim Bard.
Dealer in Words." And that was all.
I stared at the letters, whimsical
Indeed, or was it merely a jest.
He answered my unasked request:
"All books are either dreams or swords,
You can cut, or you can drug, with words.
My firm is a very ancient house,
The entries on my books would rouse
Your wonder, perhaps incredulity.
I inherited from an ancestry
Stretching remotely back and far,
This business, and my clients are
As were those of my grandfather's days,
Writers of books, and poems, and plays."

Translations

From *The Dewy Morn, Volume I, 1884* | Richard Jefferies (1848–1887)

There were books at Beechknoll such as are seldom read outside the circle of the learned, though they are books far more interesting than those of modern days. The reason the classics are not read is because there still lingers a tradition, handed down from the eighteenth century, that it is useless to read them unless in the original. A tone of sarcastic contempt is maintained towards the person who shall presume to peruse Xenophon not in the original Greek, or Virgil not in the original Latin.

. . . .

The truth is, the classics are much better understood in a good translation than in the original. To obtain a sufficient knowledge of Greek, for instance, to accurately translate is almost the work of a lifetime. Concentration upon this one pursuit gradually contracts the general perceptions, and it has often happened that an excellent scholar has been deficient in common knowledge, as shown by the singular character of his own notes. But his work of translation in itself is another matter.

It is a treasure; from it poets derive their illustrations; dramatists their plots; painters their pictures. A young mind full of intelligence, coming to such a translation, enters at once into the spirit of the ancient writer. A good translation is thus better than the original.

Lines on Tonson

John Dryden (1631–1700)

[Jacob Tonson the Elder (1655–1736) published John Dryden
and John Milton, obtained a copyright on the plays of William
Shakespeare and founded the Kit-Cat Club.]

With leering looks, bull faced, and freckled fair,
With frowsy pores poisoning the ambient air
With two left leggs, and Judas-coloured hair.

Reading Habits

From *Bookshop Memories, 1936* | George Orwell (1903–1950)

Probably our library subscribers were a fair cross-section of London's reading public. It is therefore worth noting that of all the authors in our library the one who 'went out' the best was – Priestley? Hemingway? Walpole? Wodehouse? No, Ethel M. Dell, with Warwick Deeping a good second and Jeffrey Farnol, I should say, third. Dell's novels, of course, are read solely by women, but by women of all kinds and ages and not, as one might expect, merely by wistful spinsters and the fat wives of tobacconists. It is not true that men don't read novels, but it is true that there are whole branches of fiction that they avoid. Roughly speaking, what one might call the average novel – the ordinary, good-bad, Galsworthy-and-water stuff which is the norm of the English novel – seems to exist only for women. Men read either the novels it is possible to respect, or detective stories. But their consumption of detective stories is terrific. One of our subscribers to my knowledge read four or five detective stories every week for over a year, besides others which he got from another library. What chiefly surprised me was that he never read the same book twice. Apparently the whole of that frightful torrent of trash (the pages read every year would, I calculated, cover nearly three quarters of an acre) was stored for ever in his memory. He took no notice of titles or author's names, but he could tell by merely glancing into a book whether he had 'had it already'.

On Jane Austen

Diary, 14 March 1826 | Sir Walter Scott (1771–1832)

The Big Bow-Wow strain I can do myself like any now going;
but the exquisite touch, which renders ordinary commonplace things
and characters interesting, from the truth of the description and
the sentiment, is denied me.

14 March

First Lines

From *Pride and Prejudice, 1813* | Jane Austen (1775–1817)

It is a truth universally acknowledged, that a single man in possession of a good fortune must be in want of a wife.

However little known the feelings or views of such a man may be on his first entering a neighbourhood, this truth is so well fixed in the minds of the surrounding families, that he is considered as the rightful property of some one or other of their daughters.

'My dear Mr. Bennet,' said his lady to him one day, 'have you heard that Netherfield Park is let at last?'

Mr. Bennet replied that he had not.

'But it is,' returned she; 'for Mrs. Long has just been here, and she told me all about it.'

Mr. Bennet made no answer.

'Do not you want to know who has taken it?' cried his wife impatiently.

'*You* want to tell me, and I have no objection to hearing it.'

This was invitation enough.

Paris

From *Dear Howard, 2018* | David Batterham (1933–)

March 1990

I've rediscovered Paris. Barcelona and Lisbon are all very well
for letterwriting but there are only about five shops between them.
And in any case they are both now being ruined by prosperity,
pedestrian precincts, the Olympic Games and hundreds of branches
of Benetton. Whereas in Paris there still seem to be hundreds of
bookshops and the supply of books is volcanic. Daily sales at the
Drouot, streams of runners with their green tablecloths, markets
and, I suppose, frequent deaths among old book hoarders. Of course
the quality of the lava is not what it was.

I remember coming here once during some economic crisis or
three day week in the 'seventies. Booksellers were reacting with
excessive gloom. M. Daviaud was sitting in the dark at the back of
his shop grumbling that he could only take 500F out of the country.
A man who has never once left the 6e arrondissement.

I tried to encourage M. Parrot by suggesting that if everyone was
too poor to go out to dinner or the theatre they might start buying
a lot of cheap books to read. That did cheer him up. He told me this
had happened during the war.

How Pleasant to Know ...

Edward Lear (1812–1888)

'How pleasant to know Mr. Lear!'
   Who has written such volumes of stuff!
Some think him ill-tempered and queer,
   But a few think him pleasant enough.

His mind is concrete and fastidious,
   His nose is remarkably big;
His visage is more or less hideous,
   His beard it resembles a wig.

He has ears, and two eyes, and ten fingers,
   Leastways if you reckon two thumbs;
Long ago he was one of the singers,
   But now he is one of the dumbs.

He sits in a beautiful parlour,
   With hundreds of books on the wall;
He drinks a great deal of Marsala,
   But never gets tipsy at all.

He has many friends, lay men and clerical,
    Old Foss is the name of his cat;
His body is perfectly spherical,
    He weareth a runcible hat.

When he walks in waterproof white,
    The children run after him so!
Calling out, 'He's gone out in his night-
gown, that crazy old Englishman, oh!'

He weeps by the side of the ocean,
    He weeps on the top of the hill;
He purchases pancakes and lotion,
    And chocolate shrimps from the mill.

He reads, but he cannot speak, Spanish,
    He cannot abide ginger beer:
Ere the days of his pilgrimage vanish,
    How pleasant to know Mr. Lear!

The Cause of Crime

From *The Defendant: A Defence of Penny Dreadfuls, 1901*

G. K. Chesterton (1874–1936)

It is the custom, particularly among magistrates, to attribute half the crimes of the Metropolis to cheap novelettes. If some grimy urchin runs away with an apple, the magistrate shrewdly points out that the child's knowledge that apples appease hunger is traceable to some curious literary researches. The boys themselves, when penitent, frequently accuse the novelettes with great bitterness, which is only to be expected from young people possessed of no little native humour. If I had forged a will, and could obtain sympathy by tracing the incident to the influence of Mr George Moore's novels, I should find the greatest entertainment in the diversion. At any rate, it is firmly fixed in the minds of most people that gutter-boys, unlike everybody else in the community, find their principal motives for conduct in printed books.

Now it is quite clear that this objection, the objection brought by magistrates, has nothing to do with literary merit. Bad story writing is not a crime. Mr Hall Caine walks the streets openly, and cannot be put in prison for an anticlimax. The objection rests upon the theory that the tone of the mass of boys' novelettes is criminal and degraded, appealing to low cupidity and low cruelty. This is the magisterial theory, and this is rubbish.

18 March

The Reader's Sub-conscious

From *The Reading of Books, 1946*

George Holbrook Jackson (1874–1948)

Even trivial reading has significance for the reader; and it is not only bad books which put ideas into people's heads, a reason against reading which was popular in the last century and is now as popularly used to whip the cinema. But trivial reading, like idle chatter, soothes rather than changes. The popularity of the vamp and the gangster in fiction suggests the existence of a large class of readers who are physically and acquisitively repressed, just as light reading may be a compensation for light living. Sexually starved readers are soothed by stories of vamps and lecherous he-men, as men who would like to be crooks but daren't, and those, more numerous, who have crookedness in their sub-conscious but are not likely to allow it to come to the surface, revel in works about crooks.

Necessary Editing

From *Moll Flanders: Author's Preface*, 1722

Daniel Defoe (1660–1731)

It is true that the original of this story is put into new words, and
the style of the famous lady we here speak of is a little altered;
particularly she is made to tell her own tale in modester words than
she told it at first, the copy which came first to hand having been
written in language more like one still in Newgate than one grown
penitent and humble, as she afterwards pretends to be.

The pen employed in finishing her story, and making it what you
now see it to be, has had no little difficulty to put it into a dress fit
to be seen, and to make it speak language fit to be read. When a
woman debauched from her youth, nay, even being the offspring
of debauchery and vice, comes to give an account of all her vicious
practices, and even to descend to the particular occasions and
circumstances by which she first became wicked, and of all the
progression of crime which she ran through in threescore years, an
author must be hard put to it to wrap it up so clean as not to give
room, especially for vicious readers, to turn it to his disadvantage.

All possible care, however, has been taken to give no lewd ideas,
no immodest turns in the new dressing up this story; no, not to the
worst parts of her expressions. To this purpose some of the vicious
part of her life, which could not be modestly told, is quite left out,
and several other parts are very much shortened. What is left 'tis
hoped will not offend the chastest reader or the modestest hearer; and
as the best use is made even of the worst story, the moral 'tis hoped
will keep the reader serious, even where the story might incline him
to be otherwise. To give the history of a wicked life repented of,
necessarily requires that the wicked part should be made as wicked
as the real history of it will bear, to illustrate and give a beauty to the
penitent part, which is certainly the best and brightest, if related
with equal spirit and life.

Right and Wrong

From *Tilly and the Bookwanderers*, 2018 | Anna James (1987–)

'Who's your favourite book character, Jack?' Tilly asked him as they worked.

'Tough question, Tils. And what do you mean by favourite? The character I like most, or the character I think is the best written?'

'The character you'd most like to be able to have a real-life conversation with.' Tilly replied.

'Oh, well, that's a slightly different question,' Jack said. 'The character I'd most like to talk to . . .' He paused in thought. 'I think I would be very tempted to go with Long John Silver, the pirate from *Treasure Island* – have you read that one?'

Tilly shook her head. 'I've seen the Muppet film version, though?' she offered.

Jack laughed. 'Well, I think Robert Louis Stevenson's original version is even better. Think of all the stories Silver could tell of pirates and buried treasure. Imagine the debates you could have with him.'

'He's a baddie, though, right?' Tilly asked.

'Well, yes, I suppose, technically, but the baddies are more interesting sometimes, don't you think? Or heroes who aren't always very heroic. People who do the right things for the wrong reasons or the wrong thing for the right reasons. People like Long John Silver. You should read the original.'

Poor Choices

From *The Greatness of the Soul: A Few Sighs from Hell, 1658,
1683* | John Bunyan (1628–1688)

Many a good sermon did I hear; many a time was I admonished,
desired, entreated, beseeched, threatened, forewarned, of what I now
suffer; but, alas! I was ignorant, self-conceited, surly, obstinate, and
rebellious. Many a time the preachers told me, hell would be my
portion; the devil would wreak his malice on me; God would pour
on me his sore displeasure; but he had as good have preached to
the stock, to the post, to the stones I trod on; his words rang in my
ears, but I kept them from my heart. I remember he alleged many a
scripture; but those I valued not. The scriptures, thought I, what are
they? A dead letter, a little ink and paper, of three or four shillings
price. Alas! What is the scripture? Give me a ballad, a news-book,
George on Horseback, or Bevis of Southampton. Give me some book
that teaches curious arts, that tells of old fables; but for the holy
scriptures I care not.

Books of the Hour and of All Time

From *Sesame and Lilies, 1865* | John Ruskin (1819–1900)

All books are divisible into two classes, the books of the hour, and the books of all time. Mark this distinction – it is not one of quality only. It is not merely the bad book that does not last, and the good one that does. It is a distinction of species. There are good books for the hour, and good ones for all time; bad books for the hour, and bad ones for all time.

23 March

The Heroic Novel

From *Gossip in a Library, 1891* | Edmund Gosse (1849–1928)

There is no better instance of the fact that books will not live by good works alone than is offered by the utterly neglected heroic novels of the seventeenth century. At the opening of the reign of Louis XIV in France, several writers, in the general dearth of prose fiction, began to supply the public in Paris with a series of long romances, which for at least a generation absorbed the attention of the ladies and reigned unopposed in every boudoir. I wonder whether my lady readers have ever attempted to realise how their sisters of two hundred years ago spent their time? In an English country-house of 1650, there were no magazines, no newspapers, no lawn tennis or croquet, no afternoon-teas or glee-concerts, no mothers' meetings or zenana missions, no free social intercourse with neighbours, none of the thousand and one agreeable diversions with which the life of a modern girl is diversified. On the other hand, the ladies of the house had their needlework to attend to, they had to 'stitch in a clout,' as it was called; they had to attend to the duties of a house-keeper, and, when the sun shone, they tended the garden. Perhaps they rode or drove, in a stately fashion. But through long hours they sat over their embroidery frames or mended the solemn old tapestries which lined their walls, and during these sedate performances they required a long-winded, polite, unexciting, stately book that might be read aloud by turns. The heroic novel, as provided by Gombreville, Calprenède, and Mlle de Scudéry supplied this want to perfection.

Moral or Immoral

From *The Picture of Dorian Gray: Preface, 1891*

Oscar Wilde (1854–1900)

There is no such thing as a moral or immoral book. Books are well written, or badly written. That is all.

The Condition of Books

From *Guarded by Dragons, 2021* | Rick Gekoski (1944–)

The books were in what booksellers call 'very good' condition, which means not very good – showing signs of wear throughout, but not bad enough to be described as 'good', which means terrible.

Foxing

From *The Private Library, 1897* | A. L. Humphreys (1865–1946)

Junior Assistant and later Partner, Hatchards Bookshop (1881–1924)

A fine copy should be a clean copy free from spots. When a book is spotted it is called 'foxed', and these 'foxey' books are for the most part books printed in the early part of this century, when paper-makers first discovered that they could bleach their rags and, owing to the inefficient means used to neutralise the bleach, the book carried the seeds of decay in itself, and when exposed to any damp soon became discoloured with brown stains. A foxed book cannot have the fox marks removed, and such a book should be avoided.

27 March

Thank You

From *My Name is Book: An Autobiography, 2014*

John Agard (1949–)

I, Book, can't very well tell you the story of my life without saying thank you from the bottom of my spine to all the people who make me and care about me.

To
BIBLIOPHILES for collecting me
BOOKBINDERS for binding me
BOOKSELLERS for selling me
DESIGNERS for designing me
EDITORS for editing me
ILLUSTRATORS for illustrating me
LIBRARIANS for lending me
PRINTERS for printing me
READERS for reading me
REVIEWERS for reviewing me
(favourably or not)
TRANSLATORS for translating me
WRITERS for writing me

You'll notice I mention writers last. No disrespect. That's what happens when you say things in what's called alphabetical order. Next time I'll say 'authors' instead of 'writers', so authors come first. But they won't be too upset. Writers know that somewhere it is written that the first shall be last and the last shall be first.

Safe Reading

From *Persuasion, 1818* | Jane Austen (1775–1817)

Sir Walter Elliot, of Kellynch Hall, in Somersetshire, was a man who, for his own amusement, never took up any book but the Baronetage: there he found occupation for an idle hour and consolation in a distressed one; there his faculties were roused into admiration and respect, by contemplating the limited remnant of the earliest patents; there any unwelcome sensations, arising from domestic affairs, changed naturally into pity and contempt. As he turned over the almost endless creations of the last century, and there, if every other leaf were powerless, he could read his own history with an interest which never failed. This was the page at which the favourite volume always opened:-

ELLIOT OF KELLYNCH HALL.

First Lines

From *The Great Gatsby, 1925* | F. Scott Fitzgerald (1896–1940)

In my younger and more vulnerable years my father gave me some advice that I've been turning over in my mind ever since.

'Whenever you feel like criticizing anyone,' he told me, 'just remember that all the people in this world haven't had the advantages that you've had.'

He didn't say any more, but we've always been unusually communicative in a reserved way, and I understood that he meant a great deal more than that. In consequence, I'm inclined to reserve all judgements, a habit that has opened up many curious natures to me and also made me the victim of not a few veteran bores.

30 March

Biographers

From *The Life of Samuel Johnson, 1791* | James Boswell (1740–1795)

31 March 1772

Johnson: 'Goldsmith's Life of Parnell is poor; not that it is poorly written, but that he had poor materials; for nobody can write the life of a man, but those who have eat and drunk and lived in social intercourse with him.'

I said that if it was not troublesome and presuming too much, I would request him to tell me all the little circumstances of his life; what schools he attended, when he came to Oxford, when he came to London, &c. &c. He did not disapprove of my curiosity as to these particulars; but said, 'They'll come out by degrees, as we talk together.'

APRIL

Something Sensational to Read

Explaining Poems

From *Through the Looking-Glass, and What Alice Found There, 1871, post-dated 1872* | Lewis Carroll (1832–1898)

Humpty Dumpty: 'I can explain all the poems that ever were invented – and a good many that haven't been invented just yet.'

To James Smith

Robert Burns (1759–1796)

Verse V

Some rhyme a neebor's name to lash;
Some rhyme (vain though!) for needfu' cash;
Some rhyme to court the country clash,
   An' raise a din;
For me, an aim I never fash;
   I rhyme for fun.

The Place of Poetry in a Library

From *On Books and the Housing of Them, 1890*

W. E. Gladstone (1809–1898)

I apprehend that it must take its place, the first place without doubt, in Art; for, while it is separated from Painting and her other 'sphere-born harmonious sisters' by their greater dependence on material form, they are all more inwardly and profoundly united in their first and all-enfolding principle, which is to organize the beautiful for presentation to the perceptions of man.

3 April

A Book Written on Leaves of Flowers

From *Europe: A Prophesy, 1794* | William Blake (1757–1827)

Introductory lines 14–18

Fairy:

   'I will write a book on leaves of flowers,

If you will feed me on love-thoughts, and give me now and then

A cup of sparkling poetic fancies; so, when I am tipsy,

I'll sing to you to this soft lute, and show you all alive

The World, where every particle of dust breathes forth its joy.'

4 April

The Reason for Writing

From *The Life of Samuel Johnson, 1791* | James Boswell (1740–1795)

5 April 1776

When I expressed an earnest wish for his [Samuel Johnson's] remarks on Italy, he said, 'I do not see that I could make a book upon Italy; yet I should be glad to get two hundred pounds, or five hundred pounds, by such a work.' This shewed both that a journal of his Tour upon the Continent was not wholly out of his contemplation, and that he uniformly adhered to the strange opinion which his indolent disposition made him utter: 'No man but a blockhead ever wrote, except for money.' Numerous instance to refute this will occur to all who are versed in the history of literature.

The Importance of an Index

From *The Preface, Lives of the Chief Justices of England,*
Volume III, 1857 | John, Lord Campbell (1779–1861)

I have only further to express my satisfaction in thinking that a heavy
weight is now to be removed from my conscience. So essential did
I consider an Index to be to every book, that I proposed to bring
a Bill into parliament to deprive an author who publishes a book
without an Index of the privilege of copyright; and, moreover,
to subject him, for his offence, to a pecuniary penalty. Yet, from
difficulties started by my printers, my own books have hitherto been
without an Index. But I am happy to announce that a learned friend
at the bar, on whose accuracy I can place entire reliance, has kindly
prepared a copious Index, which will be appended to this work.
Stratheden House, April 6th 1857

6 April

On Wordsworth

From *Memorial Verses, April 1850* | Matthew Arnold (1822–1888)

And Wordsworth! – Ah, pale ghosts, rejoice!
For never has such soothing voice
Been to your shadowy world convey'd,
Since erst, at morn, some wandering shade
Heard the clear song of Orpheus come
Through Hades, and the mournful gloom.
Wordsworth has gone from us – and ye,
Ah, may ye feel his voice as we!
He too upon a wintry clime
Had fallen – on this iron time
Of doubts, disputes, distractions, fears.
He found us when the age had bound
Our souls in its benumbing round;
He spoke, and loosed our heart in tears.
He laid us as we lay at birth
On the cool flowery lap of earth,
Smiles broke from us and we had ease;
The hills were round us, and the breeze
Went o'er the sun-lit fields again;
Our foreheads felt the wind and rain.
Our youth return'd; for there was shed
On spirits that had long been dead,
Spirits dried up and closely furl'd,
The freshness of the early world.

Poet, Biographer and Historian

From *Lyrical Ballads: Preface, 1802* | William Wordsworth (1770–1850)

Poetry is the image of man and nature. The obstacles which stand in the way of the fidelity of the Biographer and Historian, and of their consequent utility, are incalculably greater than those which are to be encountered by the Poet who has an adequate notion of the dignity of his art. The Poet writes under one restriction only, namely, the necessity of giving immediate pleasure to a human Being possessed of that information which may be expected from him, not as a lawyer, a physician, a mariner, an astronomer, or a natural philosopher, but as a Man. Except this one restriction, there is no object standing between the Poet and the image of things; between this, and the Biographer and Historian, there are a thousand.

8 April

A New 'Good Book'

From *Remembrance of Things Past: Within a Budding Grove,* *1924* | Marcel Proust (1871–1922) | Translated C. K. Scott Moncrieff (1889–1930)
Published in France as A *l'ombre des jeunes filles en fleurs,* 1919

A well-read man will at once begin to yawn with boredom when anyone speaks to him of a new 'good book', because he imagines a sort of composite of all the good books that he had read and knows already, whereas a good book is something special, something incalculable, and is made up not of the sum of all previous masterpieces but of something which the most thorough assimilation of every one of them would not enable him to discover, since it exists not in their sum but beyond it. Once he has become acquainted with this new work, the well-read man, till then apathetic, feels his interest awaken in the reality which it depicts.

9 April

The Queen Discovers Proust

From *The Uncommon Reader, 2006* | Alan Bennett (1934–)

[At a state banquet the president of France tells the Queen about Proust. Here she is debriefed by the foreign secretary but proves less interested in state affairs than literature.]

He [the president] had proved a mine of information about Proust, who had hitherto just been a name to the Queen. To the foreign secretary he was not even that, and so she was able to fill him in a little.

'Terrible life, poor man. A martyr to asthma, apparently, and really someone to whom one would have wanted to say, "Oh do pull your socks up." But literature's full of those. The curious thing about him was that when he dipped his cake in his tea (disgusting habit) the whole of his past life came back to him. Well, I tried it and it had no effect on me at all. The real treat when I was a child was Fuller's cakes. I suppose it might work with me if I were to taste one of them, but of course they've long since gone out of business, so no memories there. Are we finished?' She reached for her book.

The Queen's ignorance of Proust was, unlike the foreign secretary's, soon to be remedied, as Norman straightway looked him up on the internet and, finding that the novel ran to thirteen volumes, thought it would be ideal reading on Her Majesty's summer holiday at Balmoral. George Painter's biography of Proust went with them too. And seeing the blue- and pink-jacketed volumes ranged along her desk, the Queen thought they looked almost edible and straight out of a patisserie window.

10 April

Twenty Years After the First Letter

From *84 Charing Cross Road, 1971* | Helene Hanff (1916–1997)

April 11, 1969

Dear Katherine –

I take time out from housecleaning my bookshelves and sitting on the rug surrounded by books in every direction to scrawl you a Bon Voyage. I hope you and Brian have a ball in London. He said to me on the phone: 'Would you go with us if you had the fare?' and I nearly wept.

But I don't know, maybe it's just as well I never got there. I dreamed about it for so many years. I used to go to English movies just to look at the streets. I remember years ago a guy I knew told me that people going to England find exactly what they go looking for. I said I'd go looking for the England of English literature, and he nodded and said: 'It's there.'

Maybe it is, and maybe it isn't. Looking around the rug one thing's for sure: it's here.

The blessed man who sold me all the books died a few months ago. And Mr Marks who owned the shop is dead. But Marks & Co. is still there. If you happen to pass by 84 Charing Cross Road, kiss it for me! I owe it so much.

Helene

Shocking Figures

From *The Complete Polysyllabic Spree, 2006* | Nick Hornby (1957–)

April 2005

A survey conducted by W. H. Smith in 2000 found that 43 per cent
of adults questioned were unable to name a favourite book, and
45 per cent failed to come up with a favourite author. (This could
be because those questioned were unable to decide between Roth and
Bellow, but let's presume not.) Forty per cent of Britons and
43 per cent of Americans never read any books at all, of any kind.
Over the past twenty years the proportion of Americans aged 18–34
who read literature (and literature is defined as poems, plays or
narrative fiction) has fallen by 28 per cent. The 18–34 age group,
incidentally, used to be the one most likely to read a novel; it has now
become the least likely.

What Audience to Write For

From *Note-books, 1912* | Samuel Butler (1835–1902)

People between the ages of twenty and thirty read a good deal,
after thirty their reading drops off and by forty is confined to each
person's special subject, newspapers and magazines; so that the
most important part of one's audience, and that which should be
mainly written for, consists of specialists and people between twenty
and thirty.

The Argument of His Book

From *Hesperides, 1648* | Robert Herrick (1591–1674)

I sing of *Brooks*, of *Blossoms, Birds*, and *Bowers*:
Of *April, May*, of *June*, and *July*-Flowers.
I sing of *May-poles, Hock-carts, Wassails, Wakes,*
Of *Bride-grooms, Brides*, and of their *Bridall-cakes.*
I write of *Youth*, of *Love*, and have Accesse
By these, to sing of cleanly-*Wantonnesse.*
I sing of *Dewes*, of *Raines*, and piece by piece
Of *Balme*, of *Oyle*, of *Spice*, and *Amber-Greece.*
I sing of *Times trans-shifting*; and I write
How Roses first came Red, and *Lillies White.*
I write of *Groves*, of *Twilights*, and I sing
The Court of *Mab*, and of the *Fairie-King.*
I write of *Hell*; I sing (and ever shall)
Of *Heaven*, and hope to have it after all.

Where and When and How

From *The Last Essays of Elia: Detached Thoughts on Books and Reading, 1833* | Charles Lamb (1775–1834)

Much depends upon *when* and *where* you read a book. In the five or six impatient minutes, before the dinner is quite ready, who would think of taking up the *Fairy Queen* for a stop-gap, or a volume of Bishop Andrewes' sermons?

Milton almost requires a solemn service of music to be played before you enter upon him. But he brings his music – to which, who listens, had need bring docile thoughts, and purged ears.

Winter evenings – the world shut out – with less of ceremony the gentle Shakespeare enters. At such a season, the *Tempest*, or his own *Winter's Tale* – These two poets you cannot avoid reading aloud – to yourself, or (as it chances) to some single person listening. More than one – and it degenerates into an audience.

Books of quick interest, that hurry on for incidents, are for the eye to glide over only. It will not do to read them out. I could never listen to even the better kind of modern novels without extreme irksomeness.

Reading Anywhere

From *The Anatomy of Bibliomania, 1930*

George Holbrook Jackson (1874–1948)

Happy the bookman who can read anywhere, secure in his book
from all common annoyances: the tumult of traffic in cities, noise of
trains, omnibuses, automobiles, motor-cycles and pneumatic road-
drills, with their vibrant oscillations. But not all can train themselves
to endure such inconveniences: some cannot read in public or amidst
noise; and who does not prefer quietude?

16 April

The Perfect Study

From *My Books, 1823* | Leigh Hunt (1784–1859)

I do not like this fine large study. I like elegance. I like room to
breathe in, and even walk about, when I want to breathe and walk
about. I like a great library next my study; but for the study itself,
give me a small snug place, almost entirely walled with books. There
should be only one window in it, looking upon trees. Some prefer a
place with few or no books at all – nothing but a chair or a table, like
Epictetus; but I should say that these were philosophers, not lovers of
books, if I did not recollect that Montaigne was both. He had a study
in a round tower, walled as aforesaid. It is true, one forgets one's
books while writing – at least they say so. For my part, I think I have
them in a sort of side-long mind's-eye; like a second thought which is
none – like a waterfall or a whispering wind.

Litel Bok

From *Troilus and Criseyde, 1380s, Book V*

Geoffrey Chaucer (c. 1340–1400)

Go, litel bok, go, litel myn tragedie,
Ther god thy makere yet, er that he dye,
So sende might to make in som comedie!
But litel bok, no making thou n'envye,
But subgit be to alle poesye;
And kis the steppes, where-as thou seest pace
Virgile, Ovyde, Omer, Lucan, and Stace.

And for ther is so greet diversitee
In English and in wryting of our tonge,
So preye I god that non miswryte thee,
Ne thee mismetre for defaute of tonge.
And red wher-so thou be, or elles songe,
That thou be understonde, I god beseche!

Left to Posterity

From *The Diary of a Provincial Lady, 1930*

E. M. Delafield (1890–1943)

Robert says, Why don't I get into Bed? I say, Because I am writing my Diary. Robert replies, kindly, but quite definitely, that In his opinion, That is Waste of Time.

I get into bed, and am confronted by Query: Can Robert be right? Can only leave reply to Posterity.

19 April

Writing for my Own Eye

From *A Writer's Diary, 1953* | Virginia Woolf (1882–1941)

Easter Sunday, 20th April 1919

In the idleness which succeeds any long article, and Defoe is the second leader this month, I got out this diary and read, as one always does read one's own writing, with a kind of guilty intensity. I confess that the rough and random style of it, often so ungrammatical, and crying for a word altered, afflicted me somewhat. I am trying to tell whichever self it is that reads this here-after that I can write very much better; and take no time over this; and forbid her to let the eye of man behold it. And now I may add my little compliment to the effect that it has a slapdash and vigour and sometimes hits an unexpected bulls eye. But what is more to the point is my belief that the habit of writing thus for my own eye only is good practice. It loosens the ligaments. Never mind the misses and the stumbles. Going at such a pace as I do I must make the most direct and instant shots at my object, and thus have to lay hands on words, choose them and shoot them with no more pause than is needed to put my pen in the ink. I believe that during the past year I can trace some increase of ease in my professional writing which I attribute to my casual half hours after tea. Moreover there looms ahead of me the shadow of some kind of form which a diary might attain to. I might in the course of time learn what it is that one can make of this loose, drifting material of life; finding another use for it than the use I put it to, so much more consciously and scrupulously, in fiction. What sort of diary should I like mine to be? Something loose knit and yet not slovenly, so elastic that it will embrace any thing, solemn, slight or beautiful that comes into my mind. I should like it to resemble some deep old desk, or capacious hold-all, in which one flings a mass of odds and ends without looking them through.

Sensational Reading

From *The Importance of Being Earnest, 1895*

Oscar Wilde (1854–1900)

CECILY (Rather shy and confidingly): Dearest Gwendolen, there is no reason why I should make a secret of it to you. Our little county newspaper is sure to chronicle the fact next week. Mr Ernest Worthing and I are engaged to be married.

GWENDOLEN (Quite politely, rising): My darling Cecily, I think there must be some slight error. Mr Ernest Worthing is engaged to me. The announcement will appear in the *Morning Post* on Saturday at the latest.

CECILY (Very politely, rising): I am afraid you must be under some misconception. Ernest proposed to me exactly ten minutes ago. (Shows diary)

GWENDOLEN (Examines diary through her lorgnette carefully): It is certainly very curious, for he asked me to be his wife yesterday afternoon at 5.30. If you would care to verify the incident, pray do so. (Produces diary of her own) I never travel without my diary. One should always have something sensational to read in the train. I am so sorry, dear Cecily, if it is any disappointment to you, but I am afraid *I* have the prior claim.

CECILY: It would distress me more than I can tell you, dear Gwendolen, if it caused you any mental or physical anguish, but I feel bound to point out that since Ernest proposed to you he clearly has changed his mind.

Writing

William Allingham (1824–1889)

A man who keeps a diary, pays
Due toll to many tedious days;
But life becomes eventful – then
His busy hand forgets the pen.
Most books, indeed, are records less
Of fulness than of emptiness.

22 April

Being a Bookseller

From *Bookshop Memories, 1936* | George Orwell (1903–1950)

Given a good pitch and the right amount of capital, any educated person ought to be able to make a small secure living out of a bookshop. Unless one goes in for 'rare' books it is not a difficult trade to learn, and you start at a great advantage if you know anything about the insides of books. (Most booksellers don't. You can get their measure by having a look at the trade papers where they advertise their wants. If you don't see an ad. for Boswell's *Decline and Fall* you are pretty sure to see one for *The Mill on the Floss* by T. S. Eliot.) Also it is a humane trade which is not capable of being vulgarized beyond a certain point. The combines can never squeeze the small independent bookseller out of existence as they have squeezed the grocer and the milkman. But the hours of work are very long – I was only a part-time employee, but my employer put in a seventy-hour week, apart from constant expeditions out of hours to buy books – and it is an unhealthy life. As a rule a bookshop is horribly cold in winter, because if it is too warm the windows get misted over, and a bookseller lives on his windows. And books give off more and nastier dust than any other class of objects yet invented, and the top of a book is the place where every bluebottle prefers to die.

Opening a Bookshop

From *The Bookshop, 1978* | Penelope Fitzgerald (1916–2000)

[In 1959 Florence Green buys a house and warehouse in
Hardborough, on the East Anglian coast, where she intends to
open a bookshop. She goes to the bank to arrange a loan.]

'Naturally I want to reduce expenses to a minimum.' The manager
prepared to smile understandingly, but spared himself the trouble
when Florence added sharply 'But I've no intention of re-selling. It's
a peculiar thing to take a step forward in middle age, but having
done it I don't intend to retreat. What else do people think the Old
House could be used for? Why haven't they done anything about it
in the past seven years? There were jackdaws nesting in it, half the
tiles were off, it stank of rats. Wouldn't it be better as a place where
people could stand and look at books?'

'Are you talking about culture?' the manager said, in a voice half
way between pity and respect.

'Culture is for amateurs. I can't run my shop at a loss. Shakespeare
was a professional!'

It took less than it should have done to fluster Florence but at
least she had the good fortune to care deeply about something. The
manager replied soothingly that reading took up a great deal of time.

24 April

'I only wish I had more time at my disposal. People have quite the wrong ideas, you know, about the bank's closing hours. Speaking personally, I enjoy very little leisure in the evenings. But don't misunderstand me, I find a good book at my bedside of incalculable value. When I eventually retire I've no sooner read a few pages than I'm overwhelmed with sleep.'

She reflected that at this rate one good book would last the manager more than a year. The average price of a book was twelve shillings and sixpence. She sighed.

24 April

An Unusual Bookseller

From *Daniel Deronda, 1876* | George Eliot (1819–1880)

One of the shop-windows he paused before was that of a second-hand book-shop, where, on a narrow table outside, the literature of the ages was represented in judicious mixture, from the immortal verse of Homer to the mortal prose of the railway novel. That the mixture was judicious was apparent from Deronda's finding in it something that he wanted – namely, that wonderful bit of autobiography, the life of the Polish Jew, Salomon Maimon; which, as he could easily slip it into his pocket, he took from its place, and entered the shop to pay for, expecting to see behind the counter a grimy personage showing that nonchalance about sales which seems to belong universally to the second-hand book-business.

. . . .

But instead of the ordinary tradesman, he saw, on the dark background of books in the long narrow shop, a figure that was somewhat startling in its unusualness. A man in threadbare clothing, whose age was difficult to guess – from the dead yellowish flatness of the flesh, something like an old ivory carving – was seated on a stool against some book-shelves that projected beyond the short counter, doing nothing more remarkable than reading the yesterday's *Times*; but when he let the paper rest on his lap and looked at the incoming customer, the thought glanced through Deronda that precisely such a physiognomy as that might possibly have been seen in a prophet of the Exile, or in some New Hebrew poet of the mediæval time.

On *Paradise Lost*

From *Essays: Apologies for Heroic Poetry, 1677*

John Dryden (1631–1700)

One of the greatest, most noble, and most sublime poems which either this age or nation has produced.

On Mr Milton's *Paradise Lost*

Written for the second, revised edition of Paradise Lost, 1674

| Andrew Marvell (1621–1678)

When I beheld the Poet blind, yet bold,
In slender Book his vast Design unfold,
Messiah Crown'd, *God's* Reconcil'd Decree,
Rebelling *Angels*, the Forbidden Tree,
Heav'n, Hell, Earth, Chaos, All; the Argument
Held me a while misdoubting his Intent;
That he would ruine (for I saw him strong)
The sacred Truths to Fable, and old Song,
(So *Sampson* groap'd the Temples Post in spight)
The World o'rewhelming to revenge his Sight.

    Yet, as I read, soon growing less severe,
I lik'd his Project, the success did fear;
Through that wide Field how he his way should find.
O'er which lame Faith leads Understanding blind;
Lest he perplex the things he would explain,
And what was easie he should render vain.
Or if a work so infinite he spann'd,
Jealous I was that some less skilful hand
(Such as disquiet alwayes what is well,
And by ill imitating would excell)
Might hence presume the whole Creations day
To change in Scenes, and show it in a Play.

    Pardon me, *mighty Poet*, nor despise
My causeless, yet not impious surmise.
But I am now convinc'd and none will dare
Within thy Labours to pretend a Share.
Thou hast not miss'd one thought that could be fit,
And all that was improper dost omit:
So that no room is here for Writers left,
But to detect their Ignorance, or Theft.

That Majesty which through thy Work doth Reign,
Draws the Devout, deterring the Profane.
And things divine thou treast of in such state,
As them preserves, and Thee, inviolate.
At once delight and horrour on us seize,
Thou singst with so much gravity and ease;
And above human flight dost soar aloft,
With Plume so strong, so equal, and so soft.
The *Bird* nam'd from that *Paradise* you sing
So never Flags, but always keeps on Wing.
    Where couldst thou Words of such a compass find?
Whence furnish such a vast expanse of Mind?
Just Heav'n Thee, like *Tiresias*, to requite,
Rewards with *Prophecie* thy loss of Sight.
    Well might thou scorn thy Readers to allure
With Twinkling Rhime, of thy own Sense secure;
While the *Town-Bays* writes all the while and spells,
And, like a Pack-Horse tires without his Bells.
Their Fancies like our bushy Points appear,
The Poets tag them; we for fashion wear.
I, too, transported by the *Mode* offend,
And while I meant to *Praise* thee, must Commend.
Thy verse created like thy *Theme* sublime,
In Number, Weight, and Measure, needs not *Rhime*.

Deep Versed Yet Shallow

From *Paradise Regained, 1671* | John Milton (1608–1674)

Book IV, lines 318–330

Who, therefore, seeks in these
True wisdom finds her not, or, by delusion
Far worse, her false resemblance only meets,
An empty cloud. However, many books,
Wise men have said, are wearisome; who reads
Incessantly, and to his reading brings not
A spirit and judgement equal or superior,
(And what he brings what needs he elsewhere seek?)
Uncertain and unsettled still remains,
Deep versed in books and shallow in himself,
Crude or intoxicate, collecting toys
And trifles for choice matters, worth a sponge,
As children gathering pebbles on the shore.

The Books I Wanted to Write

From *Why I Write, 1946* | George Orwell (1903–1950)

When I was about sixteen I suddenly discovered the mere joy
of words, i.e. the sounds and associations of words. The lines
from *Paradise Lost,*

> So hee with difficulty and labour hard
> Moved on: with difficulty and labour hard hee,

Which do not now seem to me so very wonderful, sent shivers
down my backbone; and the spelling 'hee' for 'he' was an added
pleasure. As for the need to describe things, I knew about it already.
So it is clear what kind of books I wanted to write, in so far as
I could be said to want to write books at that time. I wanted to write
enormous naturalistic novels with unhappy endings, full of detailed
descriptions and arresting similes, and also full of purple passages in
which words were used partly for the sake of their sound. And
in fact my first complete novel, *Burmese Days*, which I wrote when
I was thirty but projected much earlier, is rather that kind of book.

Giving Books

From *The Gifts of Reading, 2016* | Robert Macfarlane (1976–)

Having been given so many astonishing books over the years, I now in turn give away as many books as I can. Birthdays, Christmases – I give books, and pretty much only books, as presents (always hard copies; I have never given, or been given, an e-book). Once or twice a year, I invite my students to my room and let them take two or three books each from several dozen that I've piled on the floor: the pleasure they take in choosing, and their disbelief that the books are *free*, reminds me of how precious books were to me when I was a student.

30 April

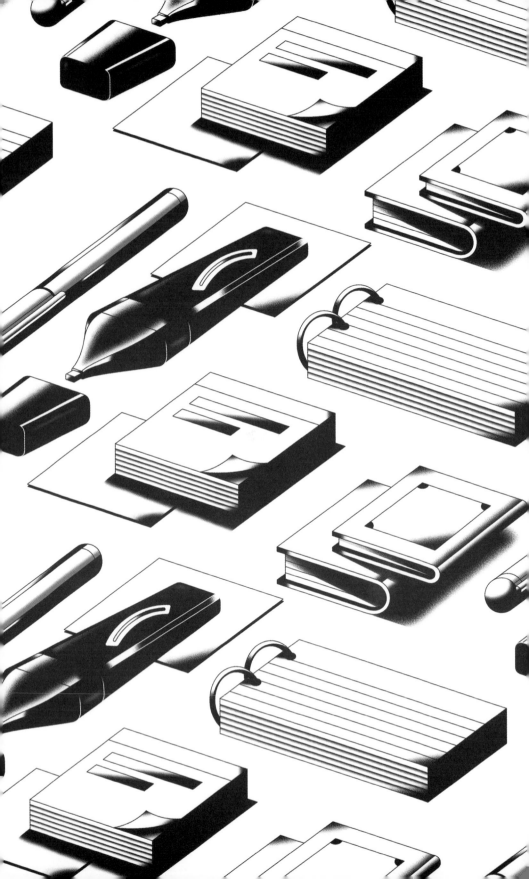

MAY

Encouraging Early Bookishness

The London Reader

From *The Life of the Fields: Country Literature*

Richard Jefferies (1848–1887)

[The Londoner] has seen books, books, books from boyhood always around him. He cannot walk down a street, enter an omnibus, go on a platform without having books thrust under his eyes. Advertisements a yard high glare at him from every hoarding, railway arch, and end-house facing a thoroughfare. In tunnels underground, on the very roofs above, book advertisements press upon his notice. It is impossible to avoid seeing them, even if he would. Books are everywhere – at home, at the reading-room, on the way to business; and on his return it is books, books, books. He buys a weekly paper, and book advertisements, book reviews, occupy a large part of it. Buy what sort of print he will – and he is always buying some sort from mere habit – books are pushed on him. If he is at all a student, or takes an interest – and what educated Londoner does not? – in some political, scientific, or other question, he is constantly on the watch for publications bearing upon it. He subscribes to or sees a copy of one or other of the purely literary papers devoted to the examination of books, and has not the slightest difficulty in finding what he wants; the reviews tell him precisely the thing he requires to know, whether the volume will suit him or not. The reading Londoner is thus in constant contact with the publisher, as much as if the publisher spoke to him across the breakfast table.

Richard Jefferies: London

From *A Literary Pilgrim in England, 1917*

Edward Thomas (1878–1917)

Though he never lived in London, Jefferies became no inconsiderable Londoner by right of a long series of visits, from the time when as a boy he used to go to the printing-house of his uncle, Thomas Harrild, in Shoe Lane. He could possess his thoughts in Trafalgar Square and under the portico of the British Museum, and, as he records in *The Story of my Heart*, he had his great moments amid the throng by the Mansion House. 'Let the grandees go to the opera,' said he in *Amaryllis*; 'for me the streets.' And he asked: 'Could Xerxes, could great Pompey, could Caesar with all his legions, could Lucullus with all his oysters, ever have enjoyed such pleasure as this, just to spend money freely in the streets of London?' And again: 'Let the meads be never so sweet, the mountain-top never so exalted, still to Fleet Street the mind will return.' He was pleased with the red roofs of Bermondsey as he saw them on approaching London Bridge by train from Eltham. He loved the ships on the Thames, and, gazing at the great red bowsprit of an Australian clipper, ridiculed the idea that Italian painters, had they seen such vessels, 'would have been contented with crank caravels and tales twice told already.' The colour of the Horse Guards, the dresses of the women, the pictures in the National Gallery, the statues in the Museum, the lions in Trafalgar Square, were among his delights.

Preface

From *Little Women, 1869* | Louisa May Alcott (1832–1888)

Go then, my little Book, and show to all
That entertain, and bid thee welcome shall,
What thou dost keep close shut up in thy breast;
And wish what thou dost show them may be blest
To them for good, may make them choose to be
Pilgrims better, by far, than thee or me.
Tell them of Mercy; she is one
Who early hath her pilgrimage begun.
Yea, let young damsels learn of her to prize
The world which is to come, and so be wise;
For little tripping maids may follow God
Along the ways which saintly feet have trod.

Adapted from John Bunyan.

3 May

Reading at Mealtimes

From *The Anatomy of Bibliomania, 1930*

George Holbrook Jackson (1874–1948)

Reading at mealtimes has innumerable precedents, and much may
be said in support of it, in spite of those who would hold fast to the
conviction that eating is an art in itself which tolerates no rival; or
those others, more medically disposed, who give out that any exigent
concern at table, by obtruding itself upon ingestion, which is the
main object, sets up a disaffection of the inward parts and ends up in
dyspepsias and other gastric derangements. But their arguments
are none too sound, and, if true, would rule out conversation and
music, and all those other amenities which add so much to the
pleasure of dining.

4 May

First Editions

From *The Bibliomania: Or, Book-Madness; Containing Some Account of the History, Symptoms, and Cure of This Fatal Disease, 1809* | Reverend Thomas Frognall Dibdin (1776–1847)

It must not, however, be forgotten that if first editions are, in some instances, of great importance, they are in many respects superfluous, and an incumbrance to the shelves of a collector; inasmuch as the labours of subsequent editors have corrected their errors, and superseded, by a great fund of additional matter, the necessity of consulting them.

5 May

To Booksellers

Message to the Booksellers of America, 6 May 1942

Franklin D. Roosevelt (1882–1945)

Books can not be killed by fire. People die, but books never die.
No man and no force can abolish memory.

. . . .

In this war, we know, books are weapons. And it is a part of your
dedication always to make them weapons for man's freedom.

6 May

155

'At Home'

From *Man of Property, 1906* | John Galsworthy (1867–1933)

George Forsyte:

The wittiest and most sportsmanlike of the Forsytes had passed
the day reading a novel in the paternal mansion at Prince's Gardens.
Since a recent crisis in his financial affairs he had been kept on parole
by Roger, and compelled to reside 'at home'.

Reading

From *Autobiography, 1883* | Anthony Trollope (1815–1882)

Reading should, no doubt, be the delight of men's leisure hours.
Had I to choose between books and cards, I should no doubt take
the books. But I find that I can seldom read with pleasure for above
an hour and a half at a time, or more than three hours a day.

The Second Book

From *The Uncommon Reader, 2006* | Alan Bennett (1934–)

[By chance, the Queen discovered the City of Westminster travelling library, run by Mr Hutchings, parked at the back of Buckingham Palace. She borrowed a book and now comes back to return it.]

She hadn't really intended to take out another book, but decided that now she was here perhaps it was easier to do it than not, though, regarding which book to choose, she felt as baffled as she had done the previous week. The truth was she didn't really want a book at all and certainly not another Ivy Compton-Burnett, which was too hard going altogether. So it was lucky that this time her eye happened to fall on a reissued volume of Nancy Mitford's *The Pursuit of Love*. She picked it up. 'Now. Didn't her sister marry the Mosley man?'

Mr Hutchings said he believed she did.

'And the mother-in-law of another sister was my mistress of the robes?'

'I don't know about that, ma'am.'

'Then of course there was the rather sad sister who had a fling with Hitler. And one became a communist. And I think there was another besides. But this is Nancy?'

'Yes, ma'am.'

'Good.'

Novels seldom come as well connected as this and the Queen felt correspondingly reassured, so it was with some confidence that she gave the book to Mr Hutchings to be stamped.

The Pursuit of Love turned out to be a fortunate choice and in its way a momentous one. Had Her Majesty gone for another duff read, an early George Eliot, say, or a late Henry James, novice reader that she was she might have been put of reading for good and there would have been no story to tell. Books, she would have thought, were work.

Pictures and Conversations

From *Alice's Adventures in Wonderland, 1865*

Lewis Carroll (1832–1898)

Alice was beginning to get very tired of sitting by her sister on the bank, and of having nothing to do: once or twice she had peeped into the book her sister was reading, but it had no pictures or conversations in it, 'and what is the use of a book,' thought Alice, 'without pictures or conversations?'

To the Gentle Reader

Andrew Lang (1844–1912)

Lines 1–5

'A French writer (whom I love well) speaks of three kinds of
companions – men, women, and books.' – Sir John Davys.

Three kinds of companions – men, women, and books,
Were enough, said the elderly sage, for his ends.
And the women we deem that he chose for their looks,
And the men for their cellars; the books were his friends:
'Man delights me not', often, 'nor woman', but books
Are the best of good comrades in loneliest nooks.

11 May

160

How to Read a Book

From *Essays: Of Studies, 1597* | Francis Bacon (1561–1626)

Some books are to be tasted, others to be swallowed, and some few to be chewed and digested. That is, some books are only to be read in parts; others to be read but cursorily; and some few to be read wholly, and with diligence and concentration.

Advice on Skipping

From *The Private Library, 1897* | Philip Gilbert Hamerton (1834–1894) |

A. L. Humphreys (1865–1946)

Junior Assistant and later Partner, Hatchards Bookshop (1881–1924)

The art of reading is a thing to learn, and with it comes the equally valuable art of skipping.

Mr Balfour's advice to readers is to learn the arts of skipping and skimming, and the late Philip Gilbert Hamerton said: – 'The art of reading is to skip judiciously. The art is to skip all that does not concern us, whilst missing nothing that we really need. No external guidance can teach this; for nobody but ourselves can guess what the needs of our intellect may be.'

The Author to Her Book

Anne Bradstreet (1612–1672)

Thou ill-formed offspring of my feeble brain,
Who after birth didst by my side remain,
Till snatched from thence by friends, less wise than true,
Who thee abroad, exposed to public view,
Made thee in rags, halting to th' press to trudge,
Where errors were not lessened (all may judge).
At thy return my blushing was not small,
My rambling brat (in print) should mother call,
I cast thee by as one unfit for light,
The visage was so irksome in my sight;
Yet being mine own, at length affection would
Thy blemishes amend, if so I could:
I washed thy face, but more defects I saw,
And rubbing off a spot still made a flaw.
I stretched thy joints to make thee even feet,
Yet still thou run'st more hobbling than is meet;
In better dress to trim thee was my mind,
But nought save homespun cloth i' th' house I find.
In this array 'mongst vulgars may'st thou roam.
In critic's hands beware thou dost not come,
And take thy way where yet thou art not known;
If for thy father asked, say thou hadst none;
And for thy mother, she alas is poor,
Which caused her thus to send thee out of door.

How to Write

From *A Swim in a Pond in the Rain*, 2021

George Saunders (1958–)

In my view, all art begins in that instant of intuitive preference.

How then to proceed? Skipping over, for the moment, the first draft, assuming some existing text to work with, my method is this: I imagine a meter mounted in my forehead, with a P on this side ('Positive') and an N on that side ('Negative'). I try to read what I've written the way a first-time reader might ('without hope and without despair'). Where's the needle? If it drops into the N zone, admit it. And then, instantaneously, a fix might present itself – a cut, a rearrangement, an addition. There's not an intellectual or analytical component to this; it's more of an impulse, one that results in a feeling of 'Ah, yes, that's better.'

. . . .

The difference between a sentence that is pleasing (that feels vivid and truthful and undeniable) and compels the reader to read the next and one that displeases her and shoots her out of the story is – well, I find I can't complete that sentence, not in a general way. And I don't need to. To be a writer, I only need to read a specific sentence of mine, in its particular context, on a given day, pencil in hand, changing the sentence as it occurs to me to do so.

Then do that again, over and over, until I'm pleased.

Roman Thoughts

Marcus Tullius Cicero (106–43BC)

Attributed and loosely translated

A room without books is like a body without a soul.

. . . .

If you have a garden and a library, you have everything you need.

. . . .

Times are bad. Children no longer obey their parents, and everyone is writing a book.

. . . .

Read at every wait; read at all hours; read within leisure; read in times of labor; read as one goes in; read as one goest out. The task of the educated mind is simply put: read to lead.

. . . .

For books are more than books, they are the life, the very heart and core of ages past, the reason why men worked and died, the essence and quintessence of their lives.

16 May

The Best Paper

From *A Note by William Morris on his Aims in Founding the Kelmscott Press, 1896* | William Morris (1834–1896)

It was a matter of course that I should consider it necessary that the paper should be hand-made, both for the sake of durability and appearance. It would be a very false economy to stint in the quality of the paper as to price: so I had only to think about the kind of hand-made paper. On this head I came to two conclusions: first, that the paper must be wholly of linen (most hand-made papers are of cotton today), and must be quite 'hard' *i.e.*, thoroughly well sized; and second, that, though it must be 'laid' and not 'wove' (*i.e.*, made on a mould made of obvious wires), the lines caused by the wires of the mould must not be too strong, so as to give a ribbed appearance. I found that on these points I was at one with the practice of the papermakers of the fifteenth century; so I took as my model a Bolognese paper of about 1473. My friend Mr Batchelor, of Little Chart, Kent, carried out my views very satisfactorily, and produced from the first the excellent paper which I still use.

There is No Frigate Like a Book

Emily Dickinson (1830–1866)

There is no Frigate like a Book
To take us Lands away
Nor any Coursers like a Page
Of prancing Poetry –
This Traverse may the poorest take
Without oppress of Toll –
How frugal is the Chariot
That bears the Human soul.

18 May

Minding Beyond Reason

From *A Room of One's Own, 1929* | Virginia Woolf (1882–1941)

Unfortunately, it is precisely the men or women of genius who mind most what is said of them. Remember Keats. Remember the words he had cut on his tombstone. Think of Tennyson; think – but I need hardly multiply instances of the undeniable, if very unfortunate, fact that it is the nature of the artist to mind excessively what is said about him. Literature is strewn with the wreckage of men who have minded beyond reason the opinions of others.

19 May

Criticism

From *Note-books, 1912* | Samuel Butler (1835–1902)

Critics generally come to be critics by reason not of their fitness for this but of their unfitness for anything else. Books should be tried by a judge and jury as though they were crimes, and counsel should be heard on both sides.

20 May

Critics

From *An Essay on Criticism, 1709* | Alexander Pope (1688–1744)

Lines 1–8

'Tis hard to say, if greater want of skill
Appear in writing or in judging ill;
But, of the two, less dang'rous is th' offence
To tire our patience, than mislead our sense.
Some few in that, but numbers err in this,
Ten censure wrong for one who writes amiss;
A fool might once himself alone expose,
Now one in verse makes many more in prose.

21 May

Children and Reading

From *News from Nowhere, 1890* | William Morris (1834–1896)

Most children, seeing books lying about, manage to read by the time they are four years old; though I am told it has not always been so.

. . . .

As a rule, they don't do much reading, except for a few story-books, till they are about fifteen years old; we don't encourage early bookishness: though you will find some children who will take to books very early; which perhaps is not good for them; but it's no use thwarting them; and very often it doesn't last long with them, and they find their level before they are twenty years old. You see, children are mostly given to imitating their elders, and when they see most people about them engaged in genuinely amusing work, like house-building and street-paving, and gardening, and the like, that is what they want to be doing; so I don't think we need fear having too many book-learned men.

On the Gift of a Book to a Child

Hilaire Belloc (1870–1953)

Child! do not throw this book about!
   Refrain from the unholy pleasure
Of cutting all the pictures out!
   Preserve it as your chiefest treasure.

Child, have you never heard it said
   That you are heir to all the ages?
Why, then, your hands were never made
   To tear these beautiful thick pages!

Your little hands were made to take
   The better things and leave the worse ones:
They also may be used to shake
   The Massive Paws of Elder Persons.

And when your prayers complete the day,
   Darling, your little tiny hands
Were also made, I think, to pray
   For men that lose their fairylands.

The English Patient's Herodotus

From *The English Patient, 1992* | Michael Ondaatje (1943–)

She picks up the notebook that lies on the small table beside his bed. It is a book he brought with him through the fire – a copy of *The Histories* by Herodotus that he has added to, cutting and gluing in pages from other books or writing in his own observations – so they are cradled within the text of Herodotus.

. . . .

She enters the painted bedroom with a new book and announces the title.

'No books now, Hana.'

She looks at him. He has, even now, she thinks, beautiful eyes. Everything occurs there, in that grey stare out of his darkness. There is a sense of numerous gazes that flicker onto her for a moment, then shift away like a lighthouse.

'No more books. Just give me Herodotus.'

She puts the thick soiled book into his hands.

'I have seen editions of *The Histories* with a sculpted portrait on the cover. Some statue found in a French museum. But I never imagined Herodotus this way. I see him more as one of those spare men of the desert who travel from oasis to oasis, trading legends as if it is the exchange of seeds, consuming everything without suspicion, piecing together a mirage. "This history of mine," Herodotus says, "has from the beginning sought out the supplementary to the main argument." What you find in him are cul-de-sacs within the sweep of history.'

Uncut Copies

From *The Bibliomania: Or, Book-Madness; Containing Some Account of the History, Symptoms, and Cure of This Fatal Disease, 1809* | Reverend Thomas Frognall Dibdin (1776–1847)

Of all the symptoms of the Bibliomania, this is probably the most extraordinary. It may be defined as a passion to possess books of which the edges have never been sheared by the binder's tools. And here, my dear Sir, I find myself walking upon doubtful ground; – your uncut Hearnes rise up in 'rough majesty' before me, and almost 'push me from my stool'. Indeed, when I look around in my book-lined tub, I cannot but be conscious that this symptom of the disorder has reached my own threshold; but when it is known that a few of my bibliographical books are left with the edges uncut *merely to please my friends* (as one must sometimes study their tastes and appetites as well as one's own), I trust that no very serious conclusions will be drawn about the probable fatality of my own case. As to uncut copies, although their inconvenience [an uncut lexicon to wit!] and deformity must be acknowledged, and although a rational man can want for nothing better than a book *once well bound* yet we find that the extraordinary passion for collecting them not only obtains with full force, but is attended with very serious consequences.

Doris's Books

From *Books and Bookmen, 1892* | Andrew Lang (1844–1912)

Doris, on your shelves I note
   Many a grave ancestral tome.
These, perhaps, you have by rote;
   These are constantly at home.
      Ah, but many a gap I spy
      Where Miss Broughton's novels lie!

Doris, there, behind the glass,
   On your Sheratonian shelves –
Oft I see them as I pass –
   Stubbs and Freeman sun themselves.
      All unread I watch them stand;
      That's *Belinda* in your hand!

Doris, I, as you may know.
   Am myself a Man of Letters,
But my learnèd volumes go
   To the top shelf, like my betters,
      High – so high that Doris could
      Scarce get at them if she would!

Doris, there be books of mine.
    That I gave you, wrote your name in,
Tooled and gilded, fair and fine:
    Don't you ever peep the same in?
        Yes, I see you've kept them – but,
        Doris, they are 'Quite Uncut!'

Quite uncut, 'unopened' rather
    Are mine edifying pages.
From this circumstance I gather
    That some other Muse engages,
        Doris, your misguided fancy:
        Yes, I thought so – reading *Nancy*.

Well, when you are *older*, Doris,
    Wiser, too, you'll love my verses;
Celia likes them, and, what more is,
    Oft – to me – their praise rehearses.
        '*Celia's Thirty*,' did I hear
        Doris, too, can be severe!

26 May

176

William Wordsworth: Guide to the Lakes

From *A Literary Pilgrim in England, 1917*

Edward Thomas (1878–1917)

It is more natural and legitimate to associate Wordsworth with
certain parts of England than any other great writer. And for three
reasons: he spent the greater portion of his life in one district; he
drew much of his scenery and human character from that district
and used its place-names very freely in his poems; and both he
and his sister left considerable records of his times and places of
composition. Moreover, he wrote a guide to the Lakes and a poem
that is not quite so useful as a guide-book, but much better.

27 May

The Tables Turned

William Wordsworth (1770–1850)

Up! up! my Friend, and quit your books;
Or surely you'll grow double:
Up! up! my Friend, and clear your looks;
Why all this toil and trouble?

The sun above the mountain's head,
A freshening lustre mellow
Through all the long green fields has spread,
His first sweet evening yellow.

Books! 'tis a dull and endless strife:
Come, hear the woodland linnet,
How sweet his music! on my life,
There's more of wisdom in it.

And hark! how blithe the throstle sings!
He, too, is no mean preacher:
Come forth into the light of things,
Let Nature be your teacher.

She has a world of ready wealth,
Our minds and hearts to bless –
Spontaneous wisdom breathed by health,
Truth breathed by cheerfulness.

One impulse from a vernal wood
May teach you more of man,
Of moral evil and of good,
Than all the sages can.

Sweet is the lore which Nature brings;
Our meddling intellect
Mis-shapes the beauteous forms of things: –
We murder to dissect.

Enough of Science and of Art;
Close up those barren leaves;
Come forth, and bring with you a heart
That watches and receives.

The Reading Room

From *The Lazy Tour of Two Idle Apprentices, 1857*

Wilkie Collins (1824–1889) | Charles Dickens (1812–1870)

29 May

[Mr Francis Goodchild and Mr Thomas Idle arrive at Allonby on the coast of Cumbria.]

In brief, it was the most delightful place ever seen.

'But,' Thomas Idle asked, 'where is it?'

'It's what you may call generally up and down the beach, here and there,' said Mr Goodchild, with a twist of his hand.

'Proceed,' said Thomas Idle.

It was, Mr Goodchild went on to say, in cross-examination, what you might call a primitive place. Large? No, it was not large. Who ever expected it would be large? Shape? What a question to ask! No shape. What sort of a street ? Why, no street. Shops? Yes, of course (quite indignant). How many? Who ever went into a place to count the shops? Ever so many.

Six? Perhaps. A library? Why, of course (indignant again). Good collection of books? Most likely – couldn't say – had seen nothing in it but a pair of scales. Any reading-room? Of course, there was a reading-room. Where? Where! why, over there. Where was over there? Why, *there*! Let Mr Idle carry his eye to that bit of waste-ground above high water-mark, where the rank grass and loose stones were most in a litter; and he would see a sort of a long ruinous brick loft, next door to a ruinous brick outhouse, which loft had a ladder outside, to get up by. That was the reading-room, and if Mr Idle didn't like the idea of a weaver's shuttle throbbing under a reading-room, that was his look-out. *He* was not to dictate, Mr Goodchild supposed (indignant again), to the company.

The Poet and His Songs

Henry Wadsworth Longfellow (1807–1882)

As the birds come in the Spring,
    We know not from where;
As the stars come at evening
    From depths of the air;

As the rain comes from the cloud,
    And the brook from the ground;
As suddenly, low or loud,
    Out of silence a sound;

As the grape comes to the vine,
    The fruit to the tree;
As the wind comes to the pine,
    And the tide to the sea;

As come the white sails of ships
    O'er the ocean's verge;
As comes the smile to the lips,
    The foam to the surge;

So come to the Poet his songs,
    All hitherward blown
From the misty realm, that belongs
    To the vast Unknown.

His, and not his, are the lays
    He sings; and their fame
Is his, and not his; and the praise
    And the pride of a name.

For voices pursue him by day,
    And haunt him by night,
And he listens, and needs must obey,
    When the Angel says: 'Write!'

When My Letters Shimmered

From *My Name is Book: An Autobiography, 2014*

John Agard (1949–)

Imagine yourself in a certain room the monks called the Scriptorium. This is where they spent devoted hours, even in the darkness of winter; for no candle was allowed, in case a precious page of parchment or vellum got caught in the flame and a scribe's handiwork that had taken years was lost in moments.

Even in those dim stone rooms, you can't imagine how Book glowed. You could say it was Book's golden period in the true sense of the word, for I was in the more than capable hands of the illuminators.

And who were these illuminators?

Mostly monks in monasteries, but also nuns in convents and professional artists.

And what exactly did these illuminators do?

Illuminate me.

With pictures that shone with colours from the juices of plants and made my pages come alive with the shimmer of gold and silver. So those who could not read and write would understand the meaning of the stories from the Bible and the lives of the saints.

They worked for long hours in silence, until my parchment began to glow, each letter a soulful stroke.

JUNE

The Poet and the Dreamer

Liking a Book

From *Gossip in a Library, 1891* | Edmund Gosse (1849–1928)

There are some books, like some people, of whom we form an
indulgent opinion without finding it easy to justify our liking.
The young man who went to the life-insurance office and reported
that his father had died of no particular disease, but just of 'plain
death', would sympathise with the feeling I mention. Sometimes we
like a book, not for any special merit, but just because it is what it is.

A Grave Sin

From *Work Suspended, 1942* | Evelyn Waugh (1903–1966)

[Mr Metcalfe arrives.]

Lady Pendlebury was in the morning room reading a novel; early training gave a guilty spice to this recreation, for she had been brought up to believe that to read a novel before luncheon was one of the gravest sins it was possible for a gentlewoman to commit. She slipped the book under a cushion and rose to greet Mr Metcalfe.

To His Books

Henry Vaughan (1621–1695)

Bright books! the perspectives to our weak sights,
The clear projections of discerning lights,
Burning and shining thoughts, man's posthume day,
The track of fled souls, and their Milky Way,
The dead alive and busy, the still voice
Of enlarg'd spirits, kind Heav'n's white decoys!
Who lives with you, lives like those knowing flow'rs,
Which in commerce with light spend all their hours;
Which shut to clouds, and shadows nicely shun,
But with glad haste unveil to kiss the sun.
Beneath you all is dark, and a dead night,
Which whoso lives in wants both health and sight.
   By sucking you, the wise, – like bees – do grow
Healing and rich, though this they do most slow,
Because most choicely: for as great a store
Have we of books, as bees of herbs, or more:
And the great task, to try, then know, the good.
To discern weeds, and judge of wholesome food,
Is a rare scant performance: for man dies
Oft ere 'tis done, while the bee feeds and flies.
But you were all choice flow'rs, all set and drest
By old sage florists, who well knew the best:
And I amidst you all am turned a weed!
Not wanting knowledge, but for want of heed.
Then thank thyself, wild fool, that wouldst not be
Content to know – what was too much for thee!

Sound Advice

Sir Herbert Maxwell (1845–1937)

A. L. Humphreys: The best advice I have ever seen in print about reading was by Sir Herbert Maxwell, and it appeared some years ago at the end of a *Nineteenth Century* article. It is as follows:

If any young person of leisure were so much at a loss as to ask advice as to what he should read, mine should be exceedingly simple – *Read anything* bearing on a definite object. Let him take up any imaginable subject to which he feels attracted, be it the precession of the equinoxes or postage stamps, the Athenian drama or London street cries; let him follow it from book to book, and unconsciously his knowledge, not of that subject only, but of many subjects, will be increased, for the departments of the realm of knowledge are divided by no *octroi*. He may abandon the first object of his pursuit for another it does not matter, one subject leads to another; he will have acquired the habit of acquisition; he will have gained that conviction of the pricelessness of time which makes it intolerable for a man to lie abed of a morning.

4 June

A Girl's Reading

From *Sesame and Lilies*, 1865 | John Ruskin (1819–1900)

Without, however, venturing here on any attempt at decision how much novel reading should be allowed, let me at least clearly assert this, – that whether novels, or poetry, or history be read, they should be chosen, not for their freedom from evil, but for their possession of good. The chance and scattered evil that may here and there haunt, or hide itself in, a powerful book, never does any harm to a noble girl; but the emptiness of an author oppresses her, and his amiable folly degrades her. And if she can have access to a good library of old and classical books, there need be no choosing at all. Keep the modern magazine and novel out of your girl's way: turn her loose into the old library every wet day, and let her alone. She will find what is good for her; you cannot: for there is just this difference between the making of a girl's character and a boy's – you may chisel a boy into shape, as you would a rock, or hammer him into it, if he be of a better kind, as you would a piece of bronze. But you cannot hammer a girl into anything. She grows as a flower does, – she will wither without sun; she will decay in her sheath; as the narcissus will, if you do not give her air enough; she may fall, and defile her head in dust, if you leave her without help at some moments of her life; but you cannot fetter her; she most take her own fair form and way, if she take any, and in mind as in body, must have always

> 'Her household motions light and free
> And steps of virgin liberty.'

Let her loose in the library, I say, as you do a fawn in a field. It knows the bad weeds twenty times better than you: and the good ones too, and will eat some bitter and prickly ones, good for it, which you had not the slightest thought would have been so.

Bookwandering

From *Tilly and the Bookwanderers, 2018* | Anna James (1987–)

[Amelia Whisper, Librarian at the British Underlibrary, explains bookwandering to Tilly and Oskar.]

'Bookwandering is the ability to travel inside books and only a very few readers can do it; you could say we read a bit harder than most people. Something tips us over from visiting the books purely inside our imaginations to being physically transported there. We still don't know precisely how it happens, and why bookwandering magic affects some people and not others. We think any reader probably has the potential to do it, but perhaps predictably there are a very high number of booksellers or librarians, as bookwanderers almost always have a very special or particular relationship with books and reading. It's this intense relationship that first starts pulling characters out of books, and why your first bookwander is normally into a book you have an affinity with – which is why it's more unusual to find out that you were also able to travel into *Anne of Green Gables*, Oskar, even though you have never read it. Pulling characters out of their stories into the real world is actually more of a side-effect, but it is almost always the way that we first realize someone has bookwandering abilities. And, as far as we can tell, bookwandering always takes place in a bookshop or library.'

A Small Drop of Ink

From *Don Juan, 1819–1824* | Lord George Gordon Byron (1788–1824)

Canto the Third

LXXXIII

But words are things, and a small drop of ink,
　Falling like dew, upon a thought, produces
That which makes thousands, perhaps millions, think;
　'Tis strange, the shortest letter which man uses
Instead of speech, may form a lasting link
　Of ages; to what straits old Time reduces
Frail man, when paper – even a rag like this,
Survives himself, his tomb, and all that's his.

LXXXIX

And when his bones are dust, his grave a blank,
　His station, generation, even his nation,
Become a thing, or nothing, save to rank
　In chronological commemoration,
Some dull MS. oblivion long has sank,
　Or graven stone found in a barrack's station
In digging the foundation of a closet,
May turn his name up, as a rare deposit.

XC

And glory long has made the sages smile;
　'Tis something, nothing, words, illusion, wind –
Depending more upon the historian's style
　Than on the name a person leaves behind:
Troy owes to Homer what whist owes to Hoyle:
　The present century was growing blind
To the great Marlborough's skill in giving knocks
Until his late Life by Archdeacon Coxe.

192

The American Protest Novel

From *Notes of a Native Son: Everybody's Protest Novel*, 1955

| James Baldwin (1924–1987)

The avowed aim of the American Protest novel is to bring greater freedom to the oppressed. They are forgiven, on the strength of these good intentions, whatever violence they do to language, whatever excessive demands they make of credibility. It is, indeed, considered the sign of a frivolity so intense as to approach decadence to suggest that these books are both badly written and wildly improbable. One is told to put first things first, the good of society coming before niceties of style or characterization. Even if this were incontestable – for what exactly is the 'good' of society? It argues an insuperable confusion, since literature and sociology are not one and the same; it is impossible to discuss them as if they were. Our passion for categorization, life neatly fitted into pegs, has led to an unforeseen, paradoxical distress, confusion, a breakdown of meaning. Those categories which were meant to define and control the world for us have boomeranged us into chaos; in which limbo we whirl, clutching the straws of our definitions. The 'protest' novel, so far from being disturbing, is an accepted and comforting aspect of the American scene, ramifying that framework we believe to be so necessary. Whatever unsettling questions are raised are evanescent, titillating, remote, for this has nothing to do with us, it is safely ensconced in the social arena, where, indeed, it has nothing to do with anyone, so that finally we receive a very definite thrill of virtue from the fact that we are reading such a book at all. This report from the pit reassures us of its reality and its darkness and of our own salvation; and 'As long as such books are being published,' an American liberal once said to me, 'everything will be all right.'

The Death of Dickens

From *Great English Novelists, 1908*

George Holbrook Jackson (1874–1948)

[Charles Dickens died on 9 June 1870.]

No other writer comes so near to the national heart as Charles Dickens. His death was treated as a national calamity, and his remains were laid in the most sacred and most honoured place in the land, the Abbey of Westminster, and to this day flowers and evergreens, and holly at the Yule Tide he did so much to make a living festival, are placed upon his grave. For three parts of a century he had served England instead of a poet, taking the place of a Burns, where a Burns was not, and of a traditional folk-muse where the ballads of the countryside were no more. Even to-day, over thirty years after his death, the charm of his books, in spite of many prognostications to the contrary, has not been worn away by the passing years. His books are still the happy reading of innumerable people wherever the English language is spoken.

An Escape into Books

From *David Copperfield, 1850* | Charles Dickens (1812–1870)

My father had left a small collection of books in a little room
upstairs, to which I had access (for it adjoined my own) and which
nobody else in our house ever troubled. From that blessed little
room, Roderick Random, Peregrine Pickle, Humphrey Clinker, Tom
Jones, the Vicar of Wakefield, Don Quixote, Gil Blas, and Robinson
Crusoe, came out, a glorious host, to keep me company. They kept
alive my fancy, and my hope of something beyond that place and
time, – they, and the Arabian Nights, and the Tales of the Genii, –
and did me no harm; for whatever harm was in some of them was not
there for me; I knew nothing of it. It is astonishing to me now, how
I found time, in the midst of my porings and blunderings over
heavier themes, to read those books as I did. It is curious to me how
I could ever have consoled myself under my small troubles (which
were great troubles to me), by impersonating my favourite characters
in them – as I did – and by putting Mr and Miss Murdstone into
all the bad ones – which I did too. I have been Tom Jones (a child's
Tom Jones, a harmless creature) for a week together. I have sustained
my own idea of Roderick Random for a month at a stretch, I verily
believe. I had a greedy relish for a few volumes of Voyages and
Travels – I forget what, now – that were on those shelves; and for
days and days I can remember to have gone about my region of our
house, armed with the centre-piece out of an old set of boot-trees
– the perfect realisation of Captain Somebody, of the Royal British
Navy, in danger of being beset by savages, and resolved to sell his life
at a great price. The Captain never lost dignity, from having his ears
boxed with the Latin Grammar. I did; but the Captain was a Captain
and a hero, in despite of all the grammars of all the languages in the
world, dead or alive.

This was my only and my constant comfort. When I think of
it, the picture always rises in my mind, of a summer evening, the
boys at play in the churchyard, and I sitting on my bed, reading as
if for life.

Books, Books, Books

From *Aurora Leigh* | Elizabeth Barrett Browning (1806–1861)

First Book, lines 832–844

Books, books, books!
I had found the secret of a garret-room
Piled high with cases in my father's name;
Piled high, packed large, – where, creeping in and out
Among the giant fossils of my past,
Like some small nimble mouse between the ribs
Of a mastodon, I nibbled here and there
At this or that box, pulling through the gap,
In heats of terror, haste, victorious joy,
The first book first. And how I felt it beat
Under my pillow, in the morning's dark,
An hour before the sun would let me read!
My books!

Double Rows

From *On Books and the Housing of Them, 1890* | W. E. Gladstone
(1809–1898)

I dispose with a passing anathema of all such as would endeavour
to solve their problem, or at any rate compromise their difficulties,
by setting one row of books in front of another.

12 June

Holiday Reading

The QI Bookshop, Turl Street, Oxford (2004–06) |
The Stockmistress / Claudia Fitzherbert (1965–)

Many years ago there was a small bookshop in Turl Street, Oxford, run by The Stockmistress (Claudia Fitzherbert). The books were shelved under unusual categories such as Informed Rants, Modest Proposals, Dislocation or Endings so you were guaranteed to find something you didn't know you were looking for. The shop has long since closed but The Stockmistress recommended a failsafe method for choosing books to read on holiday or, indeed, at any other time:

> Something old, something new,
> Something made up, something true,
> One that's here and one that's there,
> One that could be anywhere.

Seven books is about right for a week, allowing time for meals, outings and perhaps a little conversation.

Suggestions

From *A Book Lover's Holidays in the Open, 1916*

Theodore Roosevelt (1858–1919)

I am sometimes asked what books I advise men or women to take on holidays in the open. With the reservation of long trips, where bulk is of prime consequence, I can only answer: The same books one would read at home. Such an answer generally invites the further question as to what books I read when at home. To this question I am afraid my answer cannot be so instructive as it ought to be, for I have never followed any plan in reading which would apply to all persons under all circumstances; and indeed it seems to me that no plan can be laid down that will be generally applicable. If a man is not fond of books, to him reading of any kind will be drudgery. I most sincerely commiserate such a person, but I do not know how to help him. If a man or a woman is fond of books he or she will naturally seek the books that the mind and soul demand. Suggestions of a possibly helpful character can be made by outsiders, but only suggestions; and they will probably be helpful about in proportion to the outsider's knowledge of the mind and soul of the person to be helped.

14 June

Meggie's Treasure Chest

From *Inkheart, 2003* | Cornelia Funke (1958–)

Translated by Anthea Bell (1936–2018)

[Meggie and her father Mo prepare for a long journey.]

'Pack up the food and take plenty to read!' Mo called from the hall. As if she didn't always! Years ago he had made her a box to hold her favourite books on all their journeys, short and long, near and far. 'It's a good idea to have your own books with you in a strange place,' Mo always said. He himself always took at least a dozen.

Mo had painted the box poppy-red. Poppies were Meggie's favourite flower. They pressed well between the pages of a book, and you could stamp a star-shaped pattern on your skin with their pepper-pot seed capsules. He had decorated the box and painted Meggie's Treasure Chest in lovely curly lettering on the lid. The box was lined with shiny black taffeta, but you could hardly see any of the fabric because Meggie had a great many favourite books, and she always added another whenever they travelled anywhere. 'If you take a book with you on a journey,' Mo had said when he put the first one in her box, 'an odd thing happens: the book begins collecting your memories. And forever after you have only to open that book to be back where you first read it. It will all come into your mind with the very first words: the sights you saw in that place, what it smelled like, the ice cream you ate while you were reading it … yes, books are like flypapers. Memories cling to the printed page better than anything else.'

The Formation of the Roxburghe Club

The Roxburghe Club (1812–)

The Club came into existence on 16 June 1812 when a group of book-collectors and bibliophiles, inspired by the Revd Thomas Dibdin, panegyrist of Lord Spencer, the greatest collector of the age, dined together on the eve of the sale of John, Duke of Roxburghe's library, which took place on the following day. This was the greatest private library of the previous age, and the sale was confidently expected to break all records, and it did. The first edition of Boccaccio (then believed to be unique) printed in 1471 made £2,260, a record that stood for more than sixty years, and the Duke's Caxtons made equally high prices. The diners decided that this occasion should not be forgotten and so they dined again together the next year on June 17, the anniversary of the sale, and again the year after. So the Roxburghe Club was born and its members still dine together each year on, or about, that memorable day.

Size

From *Gossip in a Library, 1891* | Edmund Gosse (1849–1928)

The proverb says that a door must be either open or shut.
The bibliophile is apt to think that a book should be either
little or big. For my own part, I become more and more attached
to 'dumpy twelves'; but that does not preclude a certain discreet
fondness for folios.

The Sizes of Books

From *The Private Library, 1897* | A. L. Humphreys (1865–1946)

Junior Assistant and later Partner, Hatchards Bookshop (1881–1924)

The Associated Librarians of Great Britain decided upon a uniform and arbitrary scale for the measurement and description of the sizes of books. In consequence of the many and varied sizes of papers now manufactured, the terms folio, quarto or 4to., octavo or 8vo., twelvemo or 12mo., and so on, as indicating the number of folds in the printed sheets, can no longer be relied upon as a definite guide to the sizes of books, hence the change, as follows:

Large folio	... la. fol.	... over 18 inches
Folio	... fol.	... below 18 inches
Small folio	... sm. fol.	... below 13 inches
Large octavo	... la. 8vo.	... below 11 inches
Octavo	... 8vo.	... below 9 inches
Small octavo	... sm. 8vo.	... below 8 inches
Duodecimo	... 12mo.	... below 8 inches
Decimo octavo	... 18mo.	... is 6 inches
Minimo	... mo.	... below 6 inches
Large quarto	... la. 4to.	... below 15 inches
Quarto	... 4to.	... below 11 inches
Small quarto	... sm. 4to.	... below 8 inches

In Order

From *The Library*, 1808 | George Crabbe (1754–1832)

Lo, all in silence, all in order stand,
And mighty folios first, a lordly band;
Then quartos their well-order'd ranks maintain,
And light octavos fill a spacious plain:
See yonder, ranged in more frequented rows,
A humbler band of duodecimos;
While undistinguish'd trifles swell the scene,
The last new play and fritter'd magazine.
Thus't is in life, where first the proud, the great,
In leagued assembly keep their cumbrous state;
Heavy and huge, they fill the world with dread,
Are much admired, and are but little read:
The commons next, a middle rank, are found;
Professions fruitful pour their offspring round;
Reasoners and wits are next their place allowed,
And last, of vulgar tribes a countless crowd.

19 June

Do We Care?

From *Sesame and Lilies, 1865* | John Ruskin (1819–1900)

What do we, as a nation, care about books? How much do you think we spend altogether on our libraries, public or private, as compared with what we spend on our horses? If a man spends lavishly on his library, you call him mad – a bibliomaniac. But you never call any one a horsemaniac, though men ruin themselves every day by their horses, and you do not hear of people ruining themselves by their books. Or, to go lower still, how much do you think the contents of the book-shelves of the United Kingdom, public and private, would fetch, as compared with the contents of its wine-cellars? What position would its expenditure on literature take, as compared with its expenditure on luxurious eating? We talk of food for the mind, as of food for the body: now a good book contains such food inexhaustibly; it is a provision for life, and for the best part of us; yet how long most people would look at the best book before they would give the price of a large turbot for it?

The Cost of Reading

From *Books v. Cigarettes, 1946* | George Orwell (1903–1950)

It is difficult to establish any relationship between the price of books and the value one gets out of them. 'Books' includes novels, poetry, text books, works of reference, sociological treatises and much else, and length and price do not correspond to one another, especially if one habitually buys books second-hand. You may spend ten shillings on a poem of 500 lines, and you may spend sixpence on a dictionary which you consult at odd moments over a period of twenty years. There are books that one reads over and over again, books that become part of the furniture of one's mind and alter one's whole attitude to life, books that one dips into but never reads through, books that one reads at a single sitting and forgets a week later: and the cost, in terms of money, may be the same in each case. But if one regards reading simply as a recreation, like going to the pictures, then it is possible to make a rough estimate of what it costs. If you read nothing but novels and 'light' literature, and bought every book that you read, you would be spending – allowing eight shillings as the price of a book, and four hours as the time spent in reading it – two shillings an hour. This is about what it costs to sit in one of the more expensive seats in the cinema. If you concentrated on more serious books, and still bought everything that you read, your expenses would be about the same. The books would cost more but they would take longer to read. In either case you would still possess the books after you had read them, and they would be saleable at about a third of their purchase price. If you bought only second-hand books, your reading expenses would, of course, be much less: perhaps sixpence an hour would be a fair estimate. And on the other hand if you don't buy books, but merely borrow them from the lending library, reading costs you round about a halfpenny an hour: if you borrow them from the public library, it costs you next door to nothing.

First Lines

From *The Portrait of a Lady, 1881* | Henry James (1843–1916)

Under certain circumstances there are few hours in life more
agreeable than the hour dedicated to the ceremony known as
afternoon tea. There are circumstances in which, whether you
partake of the tea or not – some people of course never do, –
the situation is in itself delightful. Those that I have in mind in
beginning to unfold this simple history offered an admirable setting
to an innocent pastime. The implements of the little feast had been
disposed upon the lawn of an old English country-house, in what
I should call the perfect middle of a splendid summer afternoon.
Part of the afternoon had waned, but much of it was left, and what
was left was of the finest and rarest quality. Real dusk would not
arrive for many hours; but the flood of summer light had begun
to ebb, the air had grown mellow, the shadows were long upon the
smooth, dense turf. They lengthened slowly, however, and the scene
expressed that sense of leisure still to come which is perhaps the chief
source of one's enjoyment of such a scene at such an hour. From five
o'clock to eight is on certain occasions a little eternity; but on such
an occasion as this the interval could be only an eternity of pleasure.

Conclusion

From *The Defence of Poesy, written c. 1580–1581, pub. 1595*

Sir Philip Sidney (1554–1586)

So that since the ever-praiseworthy Poesy is full of virtue-breeding delightfulness, and void of no gift that ought to be in the noble name of learning; since the blames laid against it are either false or feeble; since the cause why it is not esteemed in England is the fault of poet-apes, not poets; since, lastly, our tongue is most fit to honour poesy, and to be honoured by poesy; I conjure you all that have had the evil luck to read this ink-wasting toy of mine, even in the name of the nine Muses, no more to scorn the sacred mysteries of poesy; no more to laugh at the name of poets, as though they were next inheritors to fools; no more to jest at the reverend title of a rhymer; but to believe, with Aristotle, that they were the ancient treasurers of the Grecians' divinity; to believe, with Bembus, that they were first bringers-in of all civility; to believe, with Scaliger, that no philosopher's precepts can sooner make you an honest man than the reading of Virgil; to believe, with Clauserus, the translator of Cornutus, that it pleased the Heavenly Deity by Hesiod and Homer, under the veil of fables, to give us all knowledge, logic, rhetoric, philosophy natural and moral, and *quid non?* to believe, with me, that there are many mysteries contained in poetry which of purpose were written darkly, lest by profane wits it should be abused; to believe, with Landino, that they

are so beloved of the gods, that whatsoever they write proceeds of
a divine fury; lastly, to believe themselves, when they tell you they
will make you immortal by their verses. Thus doing, your name
shall flourish in the printers' shops; thus doing, you shall be of kin
to many a poetical preface; thus doing, you shall be most fair, most
rich, most wise, most all; you shall dwell upon superlatives.

. . . .

But if (fie of such a but!) you be born so near the dull-making
cataract of Nilus, that you cannot hear the planet-like music of
poetry; if you have so earth-creeping a mind that it cannot lift
itself up to look to the sky of poetry, or rather, by a certain rustical
disdain, will become such a mome, as to be a Momus of poetry; then,
though I will not wish unto you the ass's ears of Midas, nor to be
driven by a poet's verses, as Bubonax was, to hang himself; nor to be
rhymed to death, as is said to be done in Ireland; yet thus much curse
I must send you in the behalf of all poets, that while you live in love,
and never get favour for lacking skill of a sonnet; and, when you die,
your memory die from the earth for want of an epitaph.

The Poet and the Dreamer

From *The Fall of Hyperion, Canto I* | John Keats (1791–1821)

Lines 199–202

The poet and the dreamer are distinct,
Diverse, sheer opposite, antipodes.
The one pours out a balm upon the World,
The other vexes it.

Beaune

From *Dear Howard, 2018* | David Batterham (1933–)

Dear Howard,

I like Lyon. It looks very good, like a serious town, but is more like Marshfield with its laid-back atmosphere. There are several interesting shops. M. Chartier's gets more complicated every year as he thinks up more systems to make things difficult for us. It is a huge place but he has constructed a small foyer where customers can look at a few books. Beyond this, behind him, is the vast old shop. The books are now lying on their sides, some wrapped in paper and only identifiable by a numbering system now into five figures. There is a huge old-fashioned filing cabinet with thousands of cards each covering a different subject. The files are brought out to the cubbyhole where customers rack their brains. Worse still, the prices are written in a code of letters and numbers which have to be checked against a list stuck on the wall.

M. Miraglia is more straightforward. His books are sitting there on their Remploy shelving. I wish I could buy the 15-volume surgical atlas with its stunning coloured plates for £5,000 or the vast birds-eye view of 18th century Paris for £2,500. Or even the eight volumes of coloured plates of toadstools for £1,800. They all seem rather good value but I have avoided collecting any customers rich enough to benefit from having me as a supplier. Of course it would make more sense. They are the same kind of thing that I normally deal in, just more expensive. Oh well!

Across the river in the old town, now rather ruined by pedestrian precincts and bollards, I had a very satisfying experience. Just after I arrived in the shop another customer came in and asked about magazines and was shown a pile of *La Chasse Illustrée* which I had not noticed.

I told M. Diogène in an aside that, if the other bookseller didn't take them, I would. A few minutes later I was quite shocked when the man said he'd like to buy them and M. Diogène told him they were already sold to me. I hurried into the back room in case there was a row but the poor fellow sloped off.

Love, David

Valediction of the Booke

John Donne (1572–1631)

Verses I–III

I'll tell thee now (deare Love) what thou shalt doe
    To anger destiny, as she doth us,
    How I shall stay, though she Esloygne me thus
And how posterity shall know it too;
        How thine may out-endure
        Sybills glory, and obscure
        Her who from Pindar could allure,
    And her, through whose helpe Lucan is not lame,
And her, whose booke (they say) Homer did finde, and name.

Study our manuscripts, those Myriades
    Of letters, which have past twixt thee and me,
    Thence write our Annals, and in them will bee
To all whom loves subliming fire invades,
        Rule and example found;
        There, the faith of any ground
        No schismatique will dare to wound,
    That sees, how Love this grace to us affords,
To make, to keep, to use, to be these his Records.

This Booke, as long-liv'd as the elements,
    Or as the worlds forme, this all-graved tome
    In cypher writ, or new made Idiome,
Wee for loves clergie only'are instruments:
        When this booke is made thus,
        Should againe the ravenous
        Vandals and the Goths inundate us,
    Learning were safe; in this our Universe
Schooles might learne Sciences, Spheares Musick, Angels Verse.

England

From *World of Books, 1832* | Leigh Hunt (1784–1859)

To the Editor of *Tait's Edinburgh Magazine*

Book-England on the map would shine as the Albion of the old
Giants; as the 'Logres' of the Knights of the Round Table; as the
scene of Amadis of Gaul, with its island of Windsor; as the abode
of fairies, of the Druids, of the divine Countess of Coventry, of Guy,
Earl of Warwick, of 'Alfred' (whose reality was a romance), of the
Fair Rosamond, of the Arcades and Comus, of Chaucer and Spenser,
of the poets of the Globe and the Mermaid, the wits of Twickenham
and Hampton Court. Fleet Street would be Johnson's Fleet Street;
the Tower would belong to Julius Caesar; and Blackfriars to
Suckling, Vandyke, and the Dunciad. Chronology, and the mixture
of truth and fiction, that is to say, of one sort of truth and another,
would come to nothing in a work of this kind; for, as it has been
before observed, things are real in proportion as they are impressive.
And who has not as 'gross, open, and palpable' an idea of Falstaff in
East Cheap, as of 'Captain Grose' himself; beating up his quarters?
A map of fictitious, literary, and historical London, would, of itself;
constitute a great curiosity.

The Season for Books

From *Letters from a Citizen of the World to his Friends in the East, 1760–1761* | Oliver Goldsmith (1728–1774)

Extract: Letter L

From Lien Chi Altangi to Fum Hoam, First President of the Ceremonial Academy at Pekin, in China

As I was yesterday seated at breakfast, over a pensive dish of tea, my meditations were interrupted by my old friend and companion, who introduced a stranger, dressed pretty much like himself. The gentleman made several apologies for his visit, begged of me to impute his intrusion to the sincerity of his respect, and the warmth of his curiosity.

As I am very suspicious of my company when I find them very civil without any apparent reason, I answered the stranger's caresses at first with reserve; which my friend perceiving, instantly let me into my visitant's trade and character, asking Mr Fudge, whether he had lately published any thing new? I now conjectured that my guest was no other than a bookseller, and his answer confirmed my suspicions.

'Excuse me, Sir', says he, 'it is not the season; books have their time as well as cucumbers. I would no more bring out a new work in summer, than I would sell pork in the dog-days. Nothing in my way goes off in summer, except very light goods indeed. A review, a magazine, or a sessions' paper, may amuse a summer reader; but all our stock of value we reserve for a spring and winter trade.

Nothing Quite Right

From *Mrs Dalloway, 1925* | Virginia Woolf (1882–1941)

What was she dreaming as she looked into Hatchards' shop window?
What was she trying to recover? What image of white dawn in the
country, as she read in the book spread open:

> Fear no more the heat o' the sun
> Nor the furious winter's rages.

This late age of the world's experience had bred in them all, all
men and women, a well of tears. Tears and sorrows; courage and
endurance; a perfectly upright and stoical bearing. Think, for
example, of the woman she admired most, Lady Bexborough,
opening the bazaar.

There were Jorrocks' *Jaunts and Jollities*; there were *Soapy Sponge*
and Mrs Asquith's *Memoirs* and *Big Game Shooting in Nigeria*, all
spread open. Ever so many books there were; but none that seemed
exactly right to take to Evelyn Whitbread in her nursing home.
Nothing that would serve to amuse her and make that indescribably
dried-up little woman look, as Clarissa came in, just for a moment
cordial; before they settled down for the usual interminable talk of
women's ailments.

Hatchards Bookshop

John Hatchard (1768–1849)

30 June 1797
On the opening of Hatchards Bookshop at 173 Piccadilly, London,
the oldest bookshop in London.

'This day, by the Grace of God, the goodwill of my friends and £5 in
my pocket, I have opened my shop in Piccadilly.'

JULY

I Always Took a Book

Hatchards Bookshop

From *The Books that Bind, 2018* | Mark Staples (1980–)

Some people imagine that you are a mausoleum containing dead souls, a tomb of prose. I see you as a universe. You seem to me like a living graveyard, a braveyard if you will; there's nothing spineless here. Little portals everywhere. Books are opened and closed, opened and closed like birds taking flight in slow motion, like a massively decelerated round of applause. And when you are alone, the silence – the beautiful, deafening silence. Time for reflection, in the mind and in the windows and in the mirrors and in the glass in the pictures of Virginia and Oscar. At night, we can catch a glimpse of ourselves in the first floor window and we are hovering above Piccadilly like summoned spirits.

Miles of books, a marathon of the mind. If we took all the books and piled them up vertically you could stand on the top one and spin a planet. Or you could wrap them horizontally round the world like train tracks and alight wherever you like.

Giacomo Casanova as Librarian

From *The Memoirs of Jacques Casanova de Seingalt:
Memoirs of the Prince de Ligne, 1822*

Giacomo Casanova (1725–1798) | Charles Joseph, Prince de Ligne (1735–1814)

[In 1785 Casanova became the librarian to Count Joseph Karl von
Waldstein, in the Château of Dux, Bohemia.]

Casanova, who had come to an end of his money, his travels, and his
adventures, took Waldstein at his word, and became his librarian. In
this quality he passed the last fourteen years of his life at the Château
of Dux, near Toeplitz, where for six succeeding summers he was a
constant joy to me, because of his enthusiastic liking for me, and his
useful and agreeable knowledge.

It must not be supposed, however, that he was content to live
quietly in the haven of refuge that the kindness of Waldstein had
provided for him. It was not in his nature. Not a day passed without
a storm: something was sure to be wrong with his coffee, his milk,
his dish of macaroni, which he insisted on having served to him
daily. There were constant quarrels in the house, The *chef* had spoilt
his polenta; the coachman had given him a bad driver to bring him
over to see me; the dogs had barked all night; there had been more
guests than usual, and he had been obliged to eat at a side table; a
hunting-horn had tortured his ear with discordant sounds; the *curé*
had been trying to convert him; Count Waldstein had not said good
morning to him first; the soup, out of *malice prepense*, had been
served to him too hot, or too cold; a servant had kept him waiting for

his wine; he had not been introduced to some distinguished person who had come to see the lance which pierced the side of the great Waldstein; the count had lent some one a book without telling him; a groom had not touched his hat to him; he had spoken in German and not been understood; he had got angry and people laughed at him. The fact of the matter was, that people laughed at him for many reasons. When he showed his French verses they laughed. When he declaimed Italian verses with much gesticulation, they laughed; when he came into the salon and bowed in the style which Marcel, the famous dancing-master, had taught him sixty years before, they laughed. When at all the balls he danced a minuet in a grave and stately manner, they laughed. When he put on his befeathered hat, his cloth of gold coat, his black velvet vest, his buckles with paste diamonds, worn over rolled silk stockings, they laughed.

Properly Trained Librarians

From *The Private Library, 1897* | A. L. Humphreys (1865–1946)

Junior Assistant and later Partner, Hatchards Bookshop (1881–1924)

Until we have more properly trained librarians, it is useless to recommend owners of private libraries to find a librarian, because at present there are very few such men in existence who are properly qualified. A love of books is not enough in a librarian. An orderly mind and great receptive power are most essential. Practical knowledge of bookbinding and a sense of colour are equally essential. He must have no fads of his own to be ever thrusting forward. If he is mad on Geology or Astronomy, he won't do. What, above all, he must know are the sources of information.

3 July

The Welcome

Written over an arch in Shakespeare & Co., Paris |

Shakespeare & Co. (1919–) | George Whitman (1913–2011)

Be not inhospitable to strangers lest they be angels in disguise.

From:
Be not forgetful to entertain strangers: for thereby some have
entertained angels unawares.
*The King James Bible, The Epistle of Paul the Apostle to the
Hebrews,* 13.2

4 July

224

Tobias Smollett

From *Great English Novelists, 1908*

George Holbrook Jackson (1874–1948)

Smollett, although now famous, was not well known in literary
circles and seems never to have come into the charmed circle of
Samuel Johnson. He was not by any means without friends or even
a circle of his own, and there are anecdotes left by some of his boon
fellows which show him in a pleasant and even convivial light. But
he was an ostentatious and dominant man, preferring, as is often the
case, the slavish admiration of his inferiors rather than the friendship
of his equals. His temperament was strong and self-reliant in so far as
equals and superiors went, but he liked to lean on his dependents. In
some respects this reminds one of the feudalism of Scott, who loved
nothing better than to be surrounded by retainers, but in Smollett
this love was not always free from mercenary ends. His retainers and
dependents were only too often his literary hacks and slaves.

· · · · · · · · · ·

Tobias Smollett was not a novelist whose work was essential to
English literature, and yet coming at the time it did, his work,
albeit not original in form, was a link of no small importance in the
evolution of the novel. The picaresque novel wanted the modern note,
such a note as Fielding and Richardson and Sterne had put into their
own works, and this Smollett gave to it.

· · · · · · · · · ·

Smollett is never an inseparable friend, inspiring a deep attachment
and the responsibilities of friendly relations. He is an entertaining
acquaintance. One of those good and pleasant fellows who are
known and forgotten, met casually and passed easily in the
procession of life, yet giving colour and interest to the show,
and supplying a need no less necessary and inevitable than the
great friendships.

Problems in France

From *Travels Through France and Italy, 1766*

Tobias Smollett (1721–1771)

Letter II

Boulogne sur mer, July 15, 1763

My books have been stopped at the bureau; and will be sent to
Amiens at my expense, to be examined by the *chambre syndicale*;
lest they should contain something prejudicial to the state, or to the
religion of the country. This is a species of oppression which one
would not expect to meet with in France, which piques itself on
its politeness and hospitality: but the truth is, I know no country
in which strangers are worse treated, with respect to their
essential concerns.

. . . .

[Mr B, the landlord, recommends a *requête* or petition to the
chancellor of France and recommends an *avocet* of his acquaintance.]

He composed the re*quête* in my name, which was very pompous, very
tedious, and very abject. Such a stile might perhaps be necessary in a
native of France; but I did not think it was at all suitable to a subject
of Great-Britain. I thanked him for the trouble he had taken, as he
would receive no other gratification; but when my landlord proposed
to send the memoire to his correspondent at Paris, to be delivered
to the chancellor, I told him I had changed my mind, and would
apply to the English ambassador. I have accordingly taken the liberty
to address myself to the earl of H– ; and at the same time
I have presumed to write to the duchess of D–, who is now at Paris,
to entreat her grace's advice and interposition. What effect these
applications may have, I know not: but the sieur B– shakes his
head, and has told my servant, in confidence, that I am mistaken
if I think the English ambassador is as great a man at Paris as the
chancellor of France.

Light in the British Library

From *The Life of the Fields: The Pigeons at the British Museum, 1884* | Richard Jefferies (1848–1887)

The shade deepens as I turn from the portico to the hall and vast domed house of books. The half-hearted light under the dome is stagnant and dead. For it is the nature of light to beat and throb; it has a pulse and undulation like the swing of the sea. Under the trees in the woodlands it vibrates and lives; on the hills there is a resonance of light. It beats against every leaf, and, thrown back, beats again; it is agitated with the motion of the grass blades; you can feel it ceaselessly streaming on your face. It is renewed and fresh every moment, and never twice do you see the same ray. Stayed and checked by the dome and book-built walls, the beams lose their elasticity, and the ripple ceases in the motionless pool.

7 July

The Valley of the Shadow of Books

From *New Grub Street, 1891* | George Gissing (1857–1903)

[Jasper Milvain is introduced to Miss Yule.]

'I have seen you several times. Miss Yule,' he said in a friendly way,
'though without knowing your name. It was under the great dome.'

She laughed, readily understanding his phrase.

'I am there very often,' was her reply.

'What great dome?' asked Miss Harrow, with surprise.

'That of the British Museum Reading-room,' explained Jasper;
'known to some of us as the valley of the shadow of books. People
who often work there necessarily get to know each other by sight.'

The British Museum Reading Room

Louis MacNeice (1907–1963)

Under the hive-like dome the stooping haunted readers
Go up and down the alleys, tap the cells of knowledge –
   Honey and wax, the accumulation of years –
Some on commission, some for the love of learning,
Some because they have nothing better to do
Or because they hope these walls of books will deaden
   The drumming of the demon in their ears.

Cranks, hacks, poverty-stricken scholars,
In pince-nez, period hats or romantic beards
   And cherishing their hobby or their doom
Some are too much alive and some are asleep
Hanging like bats in a world of inverted values,
Folded up in themselves in a world which is safe and silent:
   This is the British Museum Reading Room.

Out of the steps in the sun the pigeons are courting,
Puffing their ruffs and sweeping their tails or taking
   A sun-bath at their ease
And under the totem poles – the ancient terror –
Between the enormous fluted Ionic columns
There seeps from heavily jowled or hawk-like foreign faces
   The guttural sorrow of the refugees.

Bordering on the Sacred

From *The Design and Construction of the British Library,*
1998 | Colin St John Wilson (1922–2007)

There are certain types of buildings over which there hovers an aura
of myth. The most transcendent of all, the cathedral, is grounded
in the sacred so that both form and pattern of use are fused in the
language of ritual. But there is one type of building which is profane
yet in fulfilling its proper role touches the hem of the sacred: the
great library. One only has to think what crowds into the mind when
we recall the destruction of the Library in Alexandria or, akin to
that fire, the blasphemy that underlay the burning of books by Nazi
decree, for one to be made aware that the library and what it houses
embodies and protects the freedom and diversity of the human spirit
in a way that borders on the sacred.

The North Library

From *The British Museum is Falling Down, 1965*

David Lodge (1935–)

It was overheated, and its low rectangular shape and green
furnishings gave one the sense of being in an aquarium for tropical
fish. The North Library was used especially for consulting rare and
valuable books, and there were also a number of seats reserved for
the exclusive use of eminent scholars, who enjoyed the privilege of
leaving their books on their desks for indefinite periods. These desks
were rarely occupied except by piles of books and cards bearing
distinguished names, and they reminded Adam of waxworks from
which all the exhibits had been withdrawn for renovation.

11 July

True Ease in Writing

From *An Essay on Criticism, 1709* | Alexander Pope (1688–1744)

Lines 362–9

True ease in writing comes from art, not chance,
As those move easiest who have learn'd to dance.
'Tis not enough no harshness gives offence,
The sound must seem an Echo to the sense:
Soft is the strain when Zephyr gently blows,
And the smooth stream in smoother numbers flows;
But when loud surges lash the sounding shore,
The hoarse, rough verse should like the torrent roar.

English Poets

From *Letters from a Citizen of the World to his Friends in the East, 1760–1761* | Oliver Goldsmith (1728–1774)

Extract: Letter XXXIX

From Yaoua to Yaya

You have always testified the highest esteem for the English poets, and thought them not inferior to the Greeks, Romans, and even the Chinese, in the art. But it is now thought even by the English themselves, that the race of their poets is extinct; every day produces some pathetic exclamation upon the decadence of taste and genius. Pegasus, say they, has slipped the bridle from his mouth, and our modern bards attempt to direct his flight by catching him by the tail.

Yet, my friend, it is only among the ignorant that such discourses prevail; men of true discernment can see several poets still among the English, some of whom equal if not surpass their predecessors. The ignorant term that alone poetry which is couched in a certain number of syllables in every line, where a vapid thought is drawn out into a number of verses of equal length, and perhaps pointed with rhymes at the end. But glowing sentiment, striking imagery, concise expression, natural description, and modulated periods, are full sufficient entirely to fill up my idea of this art, and make way to every passion.

If my idea of poetry therefore be just, the English are not at present so destitute of poetical merit as they seem to imagine. I can see several poets in disguise among them; men furnished with the strength of soul, sublimity of sentiment, and grandeur of expression, which constitute the character. Many of the writers of their modern odes, sonnets, tragedies, or rebusses, it is true, deserve not the name, though they have done nothing but clink, rhyme, and measure syllables for years together: their Johnsons and Smollets are truly poets; though for ought I know they never made a single verse in their whole lives.

Scorn Not the Sonnet

William Wordsworth (1770–1850)

Scorn not the Sonnet; Critic, you have frowned,
Mindless of its just honours; with this key
Shakespeare unlocked his heart; the melody
Of this small lute gave ease to Petrarch's wound;
A thousand times this pipe did Tasso sound;
With it Camöens soothed an exile's grief;
The Sonnet glittered a gay myrtle leaf
Amid the cypress with which Dante crowned
His visionary brow: a glow-worm lamp,
It cheered mild Spenser, called from Faery-land
To struggle through dark ways; and, when a damp
Fell round the path of Milton, in his hand
The Thing became a trumpet; whence he blew
Soul-animating strains – alas, too few!

Choices

From *On Re-reading Novels* | Virginia Woolf (1882–1941)

Times Literary Supplement, 20th July, 1922

No writer, indeed, has so many at his disposal as a novelist. He can put himself at any point of view; he can to some extent combine several different views. He can appear in person, like Thackeray; or disappear (never perhaps completely), like Flaubert. He can state the facts, like Defoe, or give the thought without the fact, like Henry James. He can sweep the widest horizons, like Tolstoy, or seize upon one old apple-woman and her basket, like Tolstoy again.

Where there is every freedom there is every licence; and the novel, open-armed, free to all comers, claims more victims than the other forms of literature all put together. But let us look at the victors. We are tempted, indeed, to look at them a great deal more closely than space allows. For they too look different if you watch them at work. There is Thackeray always taking measures to avoid a scene, and Dickens (save in *David Copperfield*) invariably seeking one. There is Tolstoy dashing into the midst of his story without staying to lay foundations, and Balzac laying foundations so deep that the story itself seems never to begin.

Not Enough Time

From *The Reading of Books, 1946*

George Holbrook Jackson (1874–1948)

To regret that one has not enough time to read all books, or even all the best books, is useless, like regretting that one cannot visit all the desirable places of the world, or experience every exquisite sensation. Reading, like painting or sculpture, reveals its artistry at every stage. It begins but it need not end. It just stops or goes on and should suffice at every pause. All the stars and all the heavens in a page – or a sentence. Reading should be three parts gloating, dreaming, pondering upon the thing read. We all have our moments of gluttony when we can't get enough and tend to bite off more than we can chew: but to chew is best. Many books are not essential. If a book is any good you find something worth pondering on every time you open it no matter how many times you have read it.

. . . .

Good readers ruminate. To scamper through a book is like bolting your food; you miss the flavour and risk dyspepsia. There are, however, degrees of slowness. You must taste in order to assimilate. Taste is perception, assimilation understanding.

The Soul, Body and Habiliment of a Book

From *On Books and the Housing of Them, 1890*

W. E. Gladstone (1809–1898)

There is a caution which we ought to carry with us more and more as we get in view of the coming period of open book trade, and of demand practically boundless. Noble works ought not to be printed in mean and worthless forms, and cheapness ought to be limited by an instinctive sense and law of fitness. The binding of a book is the dress with which it walks out into the world. The paper, type, and ink are the body, in which its soul is domiciled. And these three, soul, body, and habiliment, are a triad which ought to be adjusted to one another by the laws of harmony and good sense.

17 July

Three Copies

Richard Heber (1773–1833)

[Richard Heber's library contained over 15,000 books and spread over eight houses. He was one of the 18 founders of the Roxburghe Club.]

No gentleman can be without three copies of a book, one for show, one for use, and one for borrowers.

Gulliver's Travels

From *Jane Eyre, 1847* | Charlotte Brontë (1816–1855)

Bessie asked if I would have a book; the word *book* acted as a
transient stimulus, and I begged her to fetch *Gulliver's Travels* from
the library. This book I had again and again perused with delight.
I considered it a narrative of facts, and discovered in it a vein of
interest deeper than what I found in fairy tales: for as to the elves,
having sought them in vain among foxglove leaves and bells, under
mushrooms, and beneath the ground-ivy mantling old wall-nooks,
I had at length made up my mind to the sad truth that they were all
gone out of England to some savage country where the woods were
wilder and thicker and the population more scant; whereas, Lilliput
and Brobdignag being, in my creed, solid parts of the earth's surface,
I doubted not that I might one day, by taking a long voyage, see
with my own eyes the little fields, houses, and trees, the diminutive
people, the tiny cows, sheep, and birds of the one realm; and the
cornfields forest-high, the mighty mastiffs, the monster cats, the
tower-like men and women of the other.

19 July

A Singular Collection of Books on Noses

From *The Life and Opinions of Tristram Shandy, 1759–1767*

Laurence Sterne (1713–1768)

My father's collection was not great, but to make amends, it was curious; and consequently he was some time in making it; he had the great good fortune however, to set off well, in getting *Bruscambille's* prologue upon long noses, almost for nothing – for he gave no more for *Bruscambille* than three half-crowns; owing indeed to the strong fancy which the stall-man saw my father had for the book the moment he laid his hands upon it. – There are not three *Bruscambilles* in Christendom – said the stall-man, except what are chain'd up in the libraries of the curious. My father flung down the money as quick as lightning – took *Bruscambille* into his bosom – hyed home from Piccadilly to Coleman-street with it, as he would have hyed home with a treasure, without taking his hand once off from *Bruscambille* all the way.

To those who do not yet know of which gender *Bruscambille* is – inasmuch as a prologue upon long noses might easily be done by either – 'twill be no objection against the simile – to say, That when my father got home, he solaced himself with *Bruscambille* after the manner in which, 'tis ten to one, your worship solaced yourself with your first mistress – that is, from morning even unto night: which, by the bye, how delightful soever it may prove to the inamorato – is of little or no entertainment at all to by-standers. – Take notice, I go no farther with the simile – my father's eye was greater than his appetite – his zeal greater than his knowledge – he cool'd – his affections became divided – he got hold of *Prignitz* – purchased *Scroderus*, Andrea *Paræus, Bouchet's* Evening Conferences, and above all, the great and learned *Hafen Slawkenbergius*.

Where My Books Go

W. B. Yeats (1865–1939)

All the words that I gather,
   And all the words that I write,
Must spread out their wings untiring,
   And never rest in their flight,
Till they come where your sad, sad heart is,
   And sing to you in the night,
Beyond where the waters are moving,
   Storm darkened or starry bright.

21 July

A Sixteenth-century Best-Seller

From *The Countess of Pembroke's Arcadia: The New Arcadia,*
1590 | Sir Philip Sidney (1554–1586)

22 July

[The Duke of Arcadia, Basilius, and his wife Gynecia:]

Of these two are brought into the world two daughters, so beyond
measure excellent in all the gifts allotted to reasonable creatures, that
we may think they were born to show that nature is no stepmother
to that sex, how much soever some men (sharp-witted only in evil
speaking) have sought to disgrace them. The elder is named Pamela;
by many men not deemed inferior to her sister: for my part, when I
marked them both, methought there was (if at least such perfection
may receive the word of more) more sweetness in Philoclea, but more
majesty in Pamela; methought love played in Philoclea's eyes, and
threatened in Pamela's; methought Philoclea's beauty only persuaded,
but so persuaded as all hearts must yield; Pamela's beauty used
violence, and such violence as no heart could resist. And it seems
that such proportion is between their minds: Philoclea so bashful,
as though her excellences had stolen into her before she was aware;
so humble, that she will put all pride out of countenance; in sum,
such proceedings as will stir hope, but teach hope good manners;
Pamela of high thoughts, who avoids not pride with not knowing her
excellences, but by making that one of her excellences, to be void of
pride; her mother's wisdom, greatness, nobility, but (if I can guess
aright) knit with a more constant temper.

An Eighteenth-century Best-Seller

From *Pamela: Or, Virtue Rewarded, Volume I, 1740*

Samuel Richardson (1689–1761)

Letter I

Dear Father and Mother,

I have great trouble, and some comfort, to acquaint you with. The
trouble is, that my good lady died of the illness I mentioned to you,
and left us all much grieved for the loss of her; for she was a dear
good lady, and kind to all us her servants. Much I feared, that as
I was taken by her ladyship to wait upon her person, I should be quite
destitute again, and forced to return to you and my poor mother,
who have enough to do to maintain yourselves; and, as my lady's
goodness had put me to write and cast accounts, and made me a little
expert at my needle, and otherwise qualified above my degree, it was
not every family that could have found a place that your poor Pamela
was fit for: but God, whose graciousness to us we have so often
experienced, put it into my good lady's heart, just an hour before
she expired, to recommend to my young master all her servants, one
by one; and when it came to my turn to be recommended (for I was
sobbing and crying at her pillow) she could only say – 'My dear son!'
and so broke off a little; and then recovering, 'remember my poor
Pamela!' And those were some of her last words. O how my eyes run!
Don't wonder to see the paper so blotted.

Well, but God's will must be done! And so comes the comfort,
that I shall not be obliged to return back to be a clog upon my dear
parents! For my master said, 'I will take care of you all, my good
maidens. And for you, Pamela,' (and took me by the hand; yes, he

took my hand before them all), 'for my dear mother's sake, I will
be a friend to you, and you shall take care of my linen.' God bless
him! and pray with me, my dear father and mother, for a blessing
upon him; for he has given mourning and a year's wages to all my
lady's servants; and I having no wages as yet (my lady having said
she would do for me as I deserved), ordered the housekeeper to give
me mourning with the rest, and gave me with his own hand four
guineas, and some silver, which were in my lady's pocket when she
died; and said, if I was a good girl, and faithful and diligent, he
would be a friend to me, for his mother's sake.

23 July

. . . .

And then he said, 'Why, Pamela, you write a very pretty hand, and
spell tolerably too. I see my good mother's care in your learning has
not been thrown away upon you. She used to say, you loved reading;
you may look into any of her books to improve yourself, so you take
care of them.' I did nothing but curtsey and cry, and was all
in confusion at his goodness. Indeed he is the best of gentlemen,
I think.

Learning to Read in America

From *Narrative of the Life of Frederick Douglass, 1845*

Frederick Douglass (1817/18–1895)

The plan which I adopted, and the one by which I was most successful, was that of making friends of all the little white boys whom I met in the street. As many of these as I could, I converted into teachers. With their kindly aid, obtained at different times and in different places, I finally succeeded in learning to read. When I was sent of errands, I always took my book with me, and by going one part of my errand quickly, I found time to get a lesson before my return. I used also to carry bread with me, enough of which was always in the house, and to which I was always welcome; for I was much better off in this regard than many of the poor white children in our neighborhood. This bread I used to bestow upon the hungry little urchins, who, in return, would give me that more valuable bread of knowledge. I am strongly tempted to give the names of two or three of those little boys, as a testimonial of the gratitude and affection I bear them; but prudence forbids; – not that it would injure me, but it might embarrass them; for it is almost an unpardonable offence to teach slaves to read in this Christian country. It is enough to say of the dear little fellows, that they lived on Philpot Street, very near Durgin and Bailey's ship-yard.

Learning to Read in Scotland

From *A Boyhood in Scotland, 1913* | John Muir (1838–1914)

I was sent to school before I had completed my third year. The first
schoolday was doubtless full of wonders, but I am not able to recall
any of them. I remember the servant washing my face and getting
soap in my eyes, and mother hanging a little green bag with my first
book in it around my neck so I would not lose it, and its blowing
back in the sea-wind like a flag. But before I was sent to school my
grandfather, as I was told, had taught me my letters from shop signs
across the street. I can remember distinctly how proud I was when
I had spelled my way through the little first book into the second,
which seemed large and important, and so on to the third. Going
from one book to another formed a grand triumphal advancement,
the memories of which still stand out in clear relief.

25 July

No Gate, No Lock, No Bolt

From *A Room of One's Own, 1929* | Virginia Woolf (1882–1941)

Literature is open to everybody. I refuse to allow you, Beadle though you are, to turn me off the grass. Lock up your libraries if you like; but there is no gate, no lock, no bolt, that you can set upon the freedom of my mind.

Out-of-doors Reading

From *The Last Essays of Elia: Detached Thoughts on Books and Reading, 1833* | Charles Lamb (1775–1834)

I am not much a friend to out-of-doors reading. I cannot settle my spirits to it. I knew a Unitarian minister, who was generally to be seen upon Snow Hill (as yet Skinner's Street was not), between the hours of ten and eleven in the morning, studying a volume of Lardner. I own this to have been a strain of abstraction beyond my reach. I used to admire how he sidled along, keeping clear of secular contacts. An illiterate encounter with a porter's knot, or a bread basket, would have quickly put to flight all the theology I am master of, and have left me worse than indifferent to the five points.

Silence

From *Gossip in a Library, 1891* | Edmund Gosse (1849–1928)

I have heard that the late Mr Edward Solly, a very pious and
worshipful lover of books, under several examples of whose book-
plate I have lately reverently placed my own, was so anxious to fly all
outward noise that he built himself a library in his garden.
I have been told that the books stood there in perfect order, with the
rose-spray flapping at the window, and great Japanese vases exhaling
such odours as most annoy an insect-nostril. The very bees would
come to the window, and sniff, and boom indignantly away again.
The silence there was perfect.

The Innkeeper's House

From *The Lazy Tour of Two Idle Apprentices, 1857*

Wilkie Collins (1824–1889) | Charles Dickens (1812–1870)

There were books, too, in this room; books on the table, books on the chimney-piece, books in an open press in the corner. Fielding was there, and Smollett was there, and Steele and Addison were there, in dispersed volumes; and there were tales of those who go down to the sea in ships, for windy nights; and there was really a choice of good books for rainy days or fine. It was so very pleasant to see these things in such a lonesome by-place – so very agreeable to find these evidences of a taste, however homely, that went beyond the beautiful cleanliness and trimness of the house – so fanciful to imagine what a wonder a room must be to the little children born in the gloomy village – what grand impressions of it those of them who became wanderers over the earth would carry away; and how, at distant ends of the world, some old voyagers would die, cherishing the belief that the finest apartment known to men was once in the Hesket-Newmarket Inn, in rare old Cumberland.

For Sale

From *Aurora Leigh* | Elizabeth Barrett Browning (1806–1861)

Book V, lines 1217–1244

At least I am a poet in being poor,
Thank God. I wonder if the manuscript
Of my long poem, if 'twere sold outright,
Would fetch enough to buy me shoes to go
Afoot (thrown in, the necessary patch
For the other side the Alps)? It cannot be.
I fear that I must sell this residue
Of my father's books, although the Elzevirs
Have fly-leaves overwritten by his hand
In faded notes as thick and fine and brown
As cobwebs on a tawny monument
Of the old Greeks – *conferenda hæc cum his* –
Corruptè citat – lege potiùs,
And so on, in the scholar's regal way
Of giving judgment on the parts of speech,
As if he sat on all twelve thrones up-piled,
Arraigning Israel. Ay, but books and notes
Must go together. And this Proclus too,
In these dear quaint contracted Grecian types,
Fantastically crumpled like his thoughts
Which would not seem too plain; you go round twice

For one step forward, then you take it back
Because you're somewhat giddy; there's the rule
For Proclus. Ah, I stained this middle leaf
With pressing in't my Florence iris-bell,
Long stalk and all: my father chided me
For that stain of blue blood, – I recollect
The peevish turn his voice took, – 'Silly girls,
Who plant their flowers in our philosophy
To make it fine, and only spoil the book!
No more of it, Aurora.' Yes – no more!
Ah, blame of love, that's sweeter than all praise
Of those who love not! 'tis so lost to me,
I cannot, in such beggared life, afford
To lose my Proclus, – not for Florence even.

The History of Books

From *The Secret Life of Books, 2019* | Tom Mole (1976–)

In its long history, the book has taken a variety of forms and employed a wide array of materials. There are books in cuneiform writing from the ancient Sumerian empire, made by pushing a stylus into clay tablets. Others were written on papyrus made from reeds growing along the Nile in ancient Egypt, or inscribed on bamboo strips in China. Books were printed from carved wooden blocks in China by 868 CE and possibly much earlier, as well as in Korea and Japan. In medieval Europe, books were written on parchment made from animal skins and decorated with coloured inks and gold leaf. Printing with metal type developed, apparently independently, in both Asia and Europe. As early as the thirteenth century, artisans at the Korean court were experimenting with copper moveable type. By the end of the fifteenth century, books were being printed in Europe using lead type to transfer ink onto paper made from linen rags.

31 July

AUGUST

Bibliomania, or Book-Madness

Ballade of the Bookman's Paradise

Andrew Lang (1844–1912)

There is a Heaven, or here, or there
A Heaven there is, for me and you.
Where bargains meet for purses spare
Like ours, are not so far and few.
Thuanus' bees go humming through
The learned groves, 'neath rainless skies.
O'er volumes old and volumes new.
    Within that Bookman's Paradise.

There, treasures bound for Longepierre
Keep brilliant their morocco blue.
There Hooke's *Amanda* is not rare,
Nor early tracts upon Peru!
Racine is common as Rotrou,
No Shakespeare quarto search defies.
And Caxtons grow as blossoms grow,
    Within that Bookman's Paradise.

There's Eve – not our first mother fair –
But Clovis Eve, a binder true;
Thither does Bauzonnet repair,
Derome, Le Gascon, Padeloup!
But never come the cropping crew
That dock a volume's honest size,
Nor they that 'letter' backs askew,
    Within that Bookman's Paradise.

ENVOY

Friend, do not Heber and de Thou,
And Scott, and Southey, kind and wise,
La chasse au bouquin still pursue
    Within that Bookman's Paradise.

The History of the Disease

From *The Bibliomania: Or, Book-Madness: Containing Some Account of the History, Symptoms, and Cure of This Fatal Disease, 1809* | Reverend Thomas Frognall Dibdin (1776–1847)

In treating of the history of this disease, it will be found to have been attended with this remarkable circumstance; namely, that it has almost uniformly confined its attacks to the male sex, and, among these, to people in the higher and middling classes of society, while the artificer, labourer, and peasant have escaped wholly uninjured. It has raged chiefly in palaces, castles, halls, and gay mansions; and those things which in general are supposed not to be inimical to health, such as cleanliness, spaciousness, and splendour, are only so many inducements towards the introduction and propagation of the Bibliomania! What renders it particularly formidable is that it rages in all seasons of the year, and at all periods of human existence. The emotions of friendship or of love are weakened or subdued as old age advances; but the influence of this passion, or rather disease, admits of no mitigation.

Dibdin's Ghost

Eugene Field (1850–1895)

Dear wife, last midnight, whilst I read
    The tomes you so despise,
A spectre rose beside the bed,
    And spake in this true wise:
'From Canaan's beatific coast
    I've come to visit thee,
For I am Frognall Dibdin's ghost,'
    Says Dibdin's ghost to me.

I bade him welcome, and we twain
    Discussed with buoyant hearts
The various things that appertain
    To bibliomaniac arts.
'Since you are fresh from t'other side,
    Pray tell me of that host
That treasured books before they died,'
    Says I to Dibdin's ghost.

'They've entered into perfect rest;
    For in the life they've won
There are no auctions to molest,
    No creditors to dun.
Their heavenly rapture has no bounds
    Beside that jasper sea;
It is a joy unknown to Lowndes,'
    Says Dibdin's ghost to me.

Much I rejoiced to hear him speak
      Of biblio-bliss above,
For I am one of those who seek
      What bibliomaniacs love.
'But tell me, for I long to hear
      What doth concern me most,
Are wives admitted to that sphere?'
      Says I to Dibdin's ghost.

'The women folk are few up there;
      For't were not fair, you know,
That they our heavenly joy should share
      Who vex us here below.
The few are those who have been kind
      To husbands such as we;
They knew our fads, and didn't mind,'
      Says Dibdin's ghost to me.

'But what of those who scold at us
      When we would read in bed?
Or, wanting victuals, make a fuss
      If we buy books instead?
And what of those who've dusted not
      Our motley pride and boast,
Shall they profane that sacred spot?'
      Says I to Dibdin's ghost.

'Oh, no! they tread that other path,
    Which leads where torments roll,
And worms, yes, bookworms, vent their wrath
    Upon the guilty soul.
Untouched of bibliomaniac grace,
    That saveth such as we,
They wallow in that dreadful place,'
    Says Dibdin's ghost to me.

'To my dear wife will I recite
    What things I've heard you say;
She'll let me read the books by night
    She's let me buy by day.
For we together by and by
    Would join that heavenly host;
She's earned a rest as well as I,'
    Says I to Dibdin's ghost.

The Oldest Society of Bibliophiles

The Roxburghe Club (1812–)

The Roxburghe Club was founded in 1812 and is the oldest society of bibliophiles in the world. Its membership is limited to 40, chosen from among those with distinguished libraries or collections, or with a scholarly interest in books. It has also been distinguished, among the many publishing societies that have done so much in this country for history, letters, antiquity and other branches of literature and art, for the quality of its publications.

These fall into two categories, both available to the public:

- Members' books: each member is expected to produce a book at his or her own expense for presentation to the other members. The subject of such books lies entirely at the discretion of the individual member, providing that it lies within the normal scope of the Club's publications.
- Club books: these are books produced by the Club itself for presentation to the members; they are also made generally available.

All books of both kinds are handsomely produced and bound in 'Roxburghe style'. Each presentation copy has the name of the member to whom it is presented in red on the list of members that usually appears at the beginning of each book.

Since its foundation, almost 300 volumes have been published on a wide range of subjects and scholarship.

Health Advice

Wendy Cope (1945–)

'People who read books enjoy a significant
"survival advantage" over those who do not.'
– report in *The Times*, 5 August 2016, on a survey
published in *Social Science and Medicine*

> If you want to stay alive,
> Sit and read a book.
> It will help you to survive.
> If you want to stay alive,
> Eat broccoli and you may thrive
> But here's the good news – look:
> If you want to stay alive,
> Sit and read a book.

5 August

Dictionaries

From *Packing My Library, 2018* | Alberto Manguel (1948–)

One of my favourite sections in the library (now in a carefully labelled box) is the one that housed my dictionaries. For my generation (I was born in the first half of the previous century) dictionaries mattered. Our elders treasured their Bible, or the complete works of Shakespeare, or Betty Crocker's cookbook, or the six volumes of the Lagarde-Michard. For generations of this third millennium, the beloved object may not be a book at all – perhaps a nostalgic Gameboy or an iPhone. But for many readers of my age, Petit Robert, Collins, Sopens, and Webster's were the names of our libraries' guardian angels. Mine, when I was in high school was the Spanish edition of the *Petit Larousse Illustré*, with its pink stratum of foreign phrases separating common words from proper names.

In the days of my youth, for those of us who liked to read, the dictionary was a magical object of mysterious powers.

The Destruction of the Great Library at Alexandria

From *The History of the Decline and Fall of the Roman Empire, 1776–1788, Volume II: 395–1185 AD*

Edward Gibbon (1737–1794)

The valuable library of Alexandria was pillaged or destroyed; and near twenty years afterwards, the appearance of the empty shelves excited the regret and indignation of every spectator whose mind was not totally darkened by religious prejudice. The compositions of ancient genius, so many of which have irretrievably perished, might surely have been excepted from the wreck of idolatry, for the amusement and instruction of succeeding ages; and either the zeal or the avarice of the archbishop might have been satiated with the rich spoils which were the reward of his victory.

7 August

Private Libraries

From *Gossip in a Library, 1891* | Edmund Gosse (1849–1928)

It is curious to reflect that the library, in our customary sense, is quite a modern institution.

Three hundred years ago there were no public libraries in Europe. The Ambrosian, at Milan, dates from 1608; the Bodleian, at Oxford, from 1612. To these Angelo Rocca added his in Rome, in 1620. But private collections of books always existed, and these were the haunts of learning, the little glimmering hearths over which knowledge spread her cold fingers, in the darkest ages of the world. To-day, although national and private munificence has increased the number of public libraries so widely that almost every reader is within reach of books, the private library still flourishes. There are men all through the civilised world to whom a book is a jewel – an individual possession of great price.

Opposition to the St Pancras Building

From *The British Library and the St Pancras Building, 1994*

Sir Anthony Kenny (1931–)

Opposition takes two forms, traditionalist and futurist. Traditionalist opposition is motivated primarily by the desire to retain in its present function the Round Reading Room in Bloomsbury. Futurist opposition is inspired by a vision that the printed book is being superseded by the computerized database.

Many people have good reason to wish for the retention of the Round Reading Room. Some are single-minded admirers of its architecture. Others are lifelong researchers who feel their work-patterns have become woven into the building.

. . . .

Futurist opposition attacks the function rather than the form of the St Pancras building. According to the futurists, the development of information technology has rendered a library as large as the St Pancras building quite superfluous. By the end of the millennium, they predict, the age of the book will have passed away, and instead of travelling to distant reading rooms, scholars and researchers will receive all the information they need at computer terminals in their own places of study.

According to the traditionalists, the new building at St Pancras is too small, its reading rooms and bookstores will need to be supplemented by the retention of Bloomsbury facilities. According to the futurists, the St Pancras building is too big: a white elephant of a construction whose miles of shelving will stand empty once the Library's holdings have all been microfilmed or digitized to bring them into the twenty-first century.

The Balbec Trees

From *Remembrance of Things Past: Cities of the Plains, 1929*

Marcel Proust (1871–1922) | Translated C. K. Scott Moncrieff (1889–1930)

When I thought that their trees, pear trees, apple trees, tamarisks,
would outlive me, I seemed to receive from them the warning
to set myself to work as last, before the hour should strike of
rest everlasting.

The Sixth Chamber Press

From *Guarded by Dragons, 2021* | Rick Gekoski (1944–)

'Private' presses come in all shapes, sizes, and incarnations. I use the term loosely to indicate what is usually a one-man show, unlikely to make its owner a living: the term 'vanity project' is irresistible. This is a floppy definition, and some imprints are hard to classify, but mine was mine alone, likely to lose money, and done just for the hell of it. Private, and as yet nameless. I had by this time tried dozens of appellations, none of which felt anything other than banal, pretentious or witless.

. . . .

William Blake, *The Marriage of Heaven and Hell*:
The first five chambers are inhabited by symbolic representations of the forces of inspiration, whirling, dangerous, dynamic, unfathomable. And then there is that sixth chamber, in which this creative wildness is tamed, organised, and reduced to the form of books, which passively sit on the shelves of libraries.

The Sixth Chamber Press! That would be the name of my new imprint. I was ever so pleased, though somewhat bemused when the purchasers of the first few books of my new imprint wondered whether the name was a reference to Russian roulette. I explained it again and again, and everyone was rather disappointed to hear my explanation. I soon commissioned a small engraving showing William Blake holding a revolver to his head, but never used it. It seemed to complicate rather than solve the problem.

A Memorable Fancy

From *The Marriage of Heaven and Hell, 1790*

William Blake (1757–1827)

I was in a Printing-house in Hell, and saw the method in which knowledge is transmitted from generation to generation.

In the first chamber was a Dragon-Man, clearing away the rubbish from a cave's mouth; within, a number of Dragons were hollowing the cave.

In the second chamber was a Viper folding round the rock and the cave, and others adorning it with gold, silver, and precious stones.

In the third chamber was an Eagle with wings and feathers of air; he caused the inside of the cave to be infinite. Around were numbers of Eagle-like men, who built palaces in the immense cliffs.

In the fourth chamber were Lions of flaming fire raging around and melting the metals into living fluids.

In the fifth chamber were Unnamed forms, which cast the metals into the expanse.

There they were received by Men who occupied the sixth chamber, and took the forms of books, and were arranged in libraries.

William Blake: Avoiding Northern Heights

From *A Literary Pilgrim in England, 1917*

Edward Thomas (1878–1917)

Blake was born and bred in London, lived there for all but three years of his life, and died there.

Nor can I discover that he ever went farther out of London, except on that one excursion to Felpham, than he could walk in a day. And he was not a walker. 'He never took walks' says Gilchrist, 'for walking's sake, or for pleasure; and could not sympathize with those who did.' Pictures, statues, and books seem to have had more reality for him than for any other man.

Merely out of books and prints, and out of his strong feeling about 'the Druid Temples which are the patriarchal pillars and oak groves,' he could probably have drawn Stonehenge so as to impress us as we are ready to be impressed after hearing about it, yet seldom are. That was one of his principal gifts, to translate into visible and chiefly human forms what would in other minds remain vague, scattered notions and fragmentary blurred images.

. . . .

It could hardly have mattered to such a man where he lived after his youth. Yet he gives as one reason for returning to London that he 'ought not to be away from the opportunities London affords of seeing fine pictures, and the various improvements in works of art going on in London'; moreover, London, and in particular South London, suited him. Towards the end of his life he complained of Hampstead air, saying that it always had been bad for him: 'When I was young, Hampstead, Highgate, Hornsey, Muswell Hill, and even Islington, and all places north of London, always laid me up the day after.' Accordingly, in London, and for much of the time near the river, he dwelt all his life, and avoided the northern heights.

To Sir Henry Goodyere

Ben Jonson (1572–1637)

Epigrammes LXXXVI

When I would know thee Goodyere, my thought lookes
Upon thy wel-made choise of friends, and bookes;
Then doe I love thee, and behold thy ends
In making thy friends bookes, and thy bookes friends:
Now, I must give thy life, and deed, the voice
Attending such a studie, such a choice.
Where, though't be love, that to thy praise doth move,
It was a knowledge, that begat that love.

A Sentimental Passion

From *Books and Bookmen, 1892* | Andrew Lang (1844–1912)

It is because the passion for books is a sentimental passion that
people who have not felt it always fail to understand it. Sentiment is
not an easy thing to explain. Englishmen especially find it impossible
to understand tastes and emotions that are not their own, – the
wrongs of Ireland, (till quite recently) the aspirations of Eastern
Roumelia, the demands of Greece. If we are to understand the book-
hunter, we must never forget that to him books are, in the first place,
relics. He likes to think that the great writers whom he admires
handled just such pages and saw such an arrangement of type as
he now beholds.

. . . .

Some rare books have these associations, and they bring you nearer
to the authors than do the modern reprints. Bibliophiles will tell you
that it is the early readings they care for, – the author's first fancies,
and those more hurried expressions which he afterwards corrected.
These readings have their literary value, especially in the masterpieces
of the great; but the sentiment after all is the main thing.

The Unpopularity of Short Stories

From *Bookshop Memories, 1936* | George Orwell (1903–1950)

Publishers get into a stew about this every two or three years.

. . . .

The kind of person who asks the librarian to choose a book for him nearly always starts by saying 'I don't want short stories', or 'I do not desire little stories', as a German customer of ours used to put it. If you ask them why, they sometimes explain that it is too much fag to get used to a new set of characters with every story; they like to 'get into' a novel which demands no further thought after the first chapter. I believe, though, that the writers are more to blame here than the readers. Most modern short stories, English and American, are utterly lifeless and worthless, far more so than most novels. The short stories which *are* stories are popular enough, vide D. H. Lawrence, whose short stories are as popular as his novels.

The House of Fiction

From *The Portrait of a Lady: Preface, 1881* | Henry James (1843–1916)
New York edition, Volume III

The house of fiction has in short not one window, but a million –
a number of possible windows not to be reckoned, rather; every one
of which has been pierced, or is still pierceable, in its vast front, by
the need of the individual vision and by the pressure of the individual
will. These apertures, of dissimilar shape and size, hang so, all
together, over the human scene that we might have expected of them
a greater sameness of report than we find. They are but windows at
the best, mere holes in a dead wall, disconnected, perched aloft; they
are not hinged doors opening straight upon life. But they have this
mark of their own that at each of them stands a figure with a pair of
eyes, or at least with a field-glass, which forms, again and again, for
observation, a unique instrument, insuring to the person making use
of it an impression distinct from every other. He and his neighbours
are watching the same show, but one seeing more where the other
sees less, one seeing black where the other sees white, one seeing big
where the other sees small, one seeing coarse where the other sees
fine. And so on, and so on; there is fortunately no saying on what,
for the particular pair of eyes, the window may not open;
'fortunately' by reason, precisely, of this incalculability of range.
The spreading field, the human scene is the 'choice of subject'; the
pierced aperture, either broad or balconied or slit-like and low-
browed, is the 'literary form'; but they are, singly or together, as
nothing without the posted presence of the watcher – without,
in other words, the consciousness of the artist.

A Novelist of the Future

From *Toys of Peace: Mark, 1919* | Saki / H. H. Munro (1870–1916)

Augustus Mellowkent was a novelist with a future; that is to say,
a limited but increasing number of people read his books, and there
seemed good reason to suppose that if he steadily continued to turn
out novels year by year a progressively increasing circle of readers
would acquire the Mellowkent habit, and demand his works from
the libraries and bookstalls. At the instigation of his publisher he had
discarded the baptismal Augustus and taken the front name of Mark.

On Taking Over as Head of Penguin

The Daily Telegraph, 19 August 1996 | Michael Lynton (1960–)

The book is the greatest interactive medium of all time. You can underline it, write in the margins, fold down a page, skip ahead. And you can take it anywhere.

Maggie Discovers Thomas à Kempis

From *The Mill on the Floss, 1860* | George Eliot (1819–1880)

The name had come across her in her reading, and she felt the
satisfaction, which every one knows, of getting some ideas to attach
to a name that strays solitary in the memory. She took up the little,
old, clumsy book with some curiosity; it had the corners turned
down in many places, and some hand, now for ever quiet, had made
at certain passages strong pen-and-ink marks, long since browned
by time. Maggie turned from leaf to leaf, and read where the quiet
hand pointed …

. . . .

A strange thrill of awe passed through Maggie while she read, as
if she had been wakened in the night by a strain of solemn music,
telling of beings whose souls had been astir while hers was in stupor.
She went on from one brown mark to another, where the quiet hand
seemed to point, hardly conscious that she was reading, seeming
rather to listen.

. . . .

She read on and on in the old book, devouring eagerly the dialogues
with the invisible Teacher, the pattern of sorrow, the source of all
strength; returning to it after she had been called away, and reading
till the sun went down behind the willows. With all the hurry of
an imagination that could never rest in the present, she sat in the
deepening twilight forming plans of self-humiliation and entire
devotedness; and in the ardour of first discovery, renunciation
seemed to her the entrance into that satisfaction which she had so
long been craving in vain.

20 August

Unusual Reading for a Little Girl

From *What Katy Did, 1872* | Susan Coolidge (1835–1905)

Katy had been sitting on the ledge of the bookcase in the Library,
poring over a book. It was called Tasso's *Jerusalem Delivered*. The
man who wrote it was an Italian, but somebody had done the story
over into English. It was rather a queer book for a little girl to take
a fancy to, but somehow Katy liked it very much. It told about
knights, and ladies, and giants, and battles, and made her feel hot
and cold by turns as she read, and as if she must rush at something,
and shout, and strike blows. Katy was naturally fond of reading.
Papa encouraged it. He kept a few books locked up, and then turned
her loose in the Library. She read all sorts of things: travels, and
sermons, and old magazines. Nothing was so dull that she couldn't
get through with it. Anything really interesting absorbed her so that
she never knew what was going on about her. The little girls to whose
houses she went visiting had found this out, and always hid away
their story-books when she was expected to tea. If they didn't do this,
she was sure to pick one up and plunge in, and then it was no use to
call her, or tug at her dress, for she neither saw nor heard anything
more, till it was time to go home.

This afternoon she read the *Jerusalem* till it was too dark to see
any more.

Biography and Autobiography

From *Minority Report: H. L. Mencken's Notebooks, 1956*

H. L. Mencken (1880–1956)

Of all the varieties of biography perhaps the most unreliable is the kind based on letters. It is rare, indeed, for a man to reveal himself, honestly and completely, to his correspondents. An account of me, based on my thousands and thousands of letters to all sorts of persons, mainly strangers, would leave out nine-tenths of my story. It would offer only occasional glimpses of my true thoughts, and in large part it would omit even my overt acts. A man seldom puts his authentic self into a letter. He writes it to amuse a friend or get rid of a social or business obligation, which is to say, a nuisance.

Autobiography, of course, is something else again. Every man writes most willingly and hence most entertainingly when writing about himself. It is the one subject that engrosses him unflaggingly, day in and day out. To be sure he almost invariably lies when he undertakes it, but his lying is of a species that is not hard to penetrate. One quickly learns what sort of impression he is trying to make, and after that it takes only a reasonable acumen to discount his evidence sufficiently. He can never quite fool a really smart reader. But his false pretences, when detected, do not spoil the interest of his story; on the contrary, they add to that interest. Every autobiography thus becomes an absorbing work of fiction, with something of the charm of a cryptogram.

Well-written or Well-spent

From *Critical and Miscellaneous Essays:*
Jean Paul Friedrich Richter, 1838 | Thomas Carlyle (1795–1881)

A well-written Life is almost as rare as a well-spent one.

A Satisfactory Day

From *Diary* | Samuel Pepys (1633–1703)

Aug. 24, 1666

Up, and despatched several businesses at home in the morning, and then comes Sympson to set up my other new presses for my books, and so he and I fell into the furnishing of my new closett, and taking out the things out of my old, and I kept him with me all day, and he dined with me, and so all the afternoon till it was quite dark hanging things, that is my maps and pictures, and draughts, and setting up my books, and as much as we could do, to my most extraordinary satisfaction.

Micro Planner and Micro Manager: Two Breeds of Novelist

From *That Crafty Feeling*, 2009 | Zadie Smith (1975–)

You will recognise a Macro Planner from his Post-its, from those Moleskins he insists on buying. A Macro Planner makes notes, organizes material, configures a plot and creates a structure – all before he writes the title page. This structural security gives him a great deal of freedom of movement. It's not uncommon for Macro Planners to start writing their novels in the middle. As they progress, forwards or backwards, their difficulties multiply with their choices. I know Macro Planners who obsessively exchange possible endings for one another, who take characters out and then put them back in, reverse the order of chapters and perform frequent – for me, unthinkable – radical surgery on their novels: moving the setting of a book from London to Berlin, for example, or changing the title. I can't stand to hear them speak about all this, not because I disapprove, but because other people's methods are always so incomprehensible and horrifying. I am a Micro Manager. I start at the first sentence of a novel and I finish at the last. It would never occur to me to choose between three different endings because I haven't the slightest idea of the ending until I get to it, a fact that will surprise no one who has read my novels. Macro Planners have their houses largely built from day one, and so their obsession is internal – they're forever moving the furniture. They'll put a chair in the bedroom, the lounge, the kitchen and then back in the bedroom again. Micro Managers build a house floor by floor, discretely and in its entirety. Each floor needs to be sturdy and fully decorated with all the furniture in place before the next is built on top of it. There's wallpaper in the hall even if the stairs lead nowhere at all.

The Importance of Experience

From *The Private Library, 1897* | A. L. Humphreys (1865–1946)

Junior Assistant and later Partner, Hatchards Bookshop (1881–1924)

It would be impossible to tell all the causes which go towards determining the value of a book and which cause it to fluctuate in price. There is but one way to arrive at a reliable knowledge of book values, and that is to begin stall-hunting as soon as you leave school or college and continue until past middle age, absorbing information from stalls, from catalogues, and from sale-rooms. The records of prices at which books have been sold in the auction rooms, and which are regularly issued, are useless in the hands of an inexperienced person. To make up your mind on Monday that you are going to begin a career of successful bargain-hunting and book-collecting is only to be defrauded on all the other five remaining days. Experience must be bought, and an eye for a good copy of a book, or for a bargain of any kind, only comes after years of practice.

Bookshops and Catalogues

From *Unpacking My Library, 1931* | Walter Benjamin (1892–1940)

[We] reach the wide highway of book acquisition, namely, the purchasing of books. This is indeed a wide highway, but not a comfortable one. The purchasing done by a book collector has very little in common with that done in a bookshop by a student getting a text-book, a man of the world buying a present for his lady, or a businessman intending to while away his next train journey. I have made my most memorable purchases on trips, as a transient. Property and possession belong to the tactical sphere. Collectors are people with a tactical instinct; their experience teaches them that when they capture a strange city, the smallest antique shop can be a fortress, the most remote stationery store a key position. How many cities have revealed themselves to me in the marches I undertook in the pursuit of books!

By no means all of the most important purchases are made on the premises of a dealer. Catalogues play a far greater part. And even though the purchaser may be thoroughly acquainted with the book ordered from a catalogue, the individual copy always remains a surprise and the order always a bit of a gamble. There are grievous disappointments, but also happy finds.

Amusing or Dull

From *The Vicar of Wakefield, 1761–1762, published 1766*

Oliver Goldsmith (1730–1774)

There are an hundred faults in this Thing, and an hundred things
might be said to prove them beauties. But it is needless. A book may
be amusing with numerous errors, or it may be very dull without a
single absurdity. The hero of this piece unites in himself the three
greatest characters upon earth; he is a priest, an husbandman, and
the father of a family. He is drawn as ready to teach, and ready to
obey, as simple in affluence, and majestic in adversity. In this age of
opulence and refinement whom can such a character please? Such as
are fond of high life, will turn with disdain from the simplicity of
his country fire-side. Such as mistake ribaldry for humour, will find
no wit in his harmless conversation; and such as have been taught to
deride religion, will laugh at one whose chief stores of comfort are
drawn from futurity.

A Munificent Gift

From *Diary* | John Evelyn (1620–1706)

29th August, 1678

I was called to London to wait upon the Duke of Norfolk, who
having at my sole request bestowed the Arundelian Library on the
Royal Society, sent to me to take charge of the books and remove
them, only stipulating that I would suffer the Herald's chief officer,
Sir William Dugdale, to have such of them as concerned Heraldry
and the Marshal's office, books of Armory and Genealogies, the
Duke being Earl Marshal of England. I procured for our Society,
besides printed books, near one hundred MSS., some in Greek
of great concernment. The printed books, being of the oldest
impressions, are not the less valuable; I esteem them almost equal
to MSS. Amongst them, are most of the Fathers, printed at Basil,
before the Jesuits abused them with their expurgatory Indexes; there
is a noble MS. of Vitruvius. Many of these books had been presented
by Popes, Cardinals and great persons, to the Earls of Arundel and
Dukes of Norfolk; and the late magnificent Earl of Arundel bought
a noble library in Germany, which is in this collection. I should not,
for the honour I bear the family, have persuaded the Duke to part
with these, had I not seen how negligent he was of them, suffering
the priests and everybody to carry away and dispose of what they
pleased; so that abundance of rare things are irrecoverably gone.

Having taken order here, I went to the Royal Society to give
them an account of what I had procured, that they might call a
Council and appoint a day to wait on the Duke to thank him for
this munificent gift.

The Love of Books in France

From *Books and Bookmen, 1892* | Andrew Lang (1844–1912)

The love of books for their own sake, for their paper, print, binding, and for their associations, as distinct from the love of literature, is a stronger and more universal passion in France than elsewhere in Europe. In England publishers are men of business; in France they aspire to be artists. In England people borrow what they read from the libraries, and take what gaudy cloth-binding chance chooses to send them. In France people buy books, and bind them to their heart's desire with quaint and dainty devices on the morocco covers. Books are lifelong friends in that country; in England they are the guests of a week or of a fortnight.

Dear Old London

Eugene Field (1850–1895)

Verse I

When I was broke in London in the fall of '89,
I chanced to spy in Oxford Street this tantalizing sign, –
'A Splendid Horace cheap for Cash!' Of course I had to look
Upon the vaunted bargain, and it was a noble book!
A finer one I've never seen, nor can I hope to see, –
The first edition, richly bound, and clean as clean can be;
And, just to think, for three-pounds-ten I might have had that Pine,
When I was broke in London in the fall of '89!

SEPTEMBER

In an Elbow-Chair at Ease

Shut Not Your Doors

Walt Whitman (1819–1892)

Shut not your doors to me proud libraries,
For that which was lacking on all your well-fill'd shelves,
    yet needed most, I bring,
Forth from the war emerging, a book I have made,
The words of my book nothing, the drift of it every thing,
A book separate, not link'd with the rest nor felt by the intellect,
But you ye untold latencies will thrill to every page.

Poisonous Slanderers

From *Tom Jones, 1749* | Henry Fielding (1707–1854)

The author whose muse hath brought forth, will feel the pathetic strain, perhaps will accompany me with tears (especially if his darling be already no more) while I mention the uneasiness with which the big muse bears about her burden, the painful labour with which she produces it, and lastly, the care, the fondness, with which the tender father nourishes his favourite, till it be brought to maturity, and produced into the world.

Nor is there any paternal fondness which seems less to savour of absolute instinct, and which may so well be reconciled to worldly wisdom, as this. These children may most truly be called the riches of their father; and many of them have with true filial piety fed their parent in his old age; so that not only the affection, but the interest of the author may be highly injured by these slanderers, whose poisonous breath brings his book to an untimely end.

Caring for Books

From *The Enemies of Books, 1880* | William Blades (1824–1890)

The surest way to preserve your books in health is to treat them as you should your own children, who are sure to sicken if confined in an atmosphere which is impure, too hot, too cold, too damp, or too dry. It is just the same with the progeny of literature.

Books and Children

From *Note-books, 1912* | Samuel Butler (1835–1902)

If the literary offspring is not to die young, almost as much trouble must be taken with it as with the bringing up of a physical child. Still, the physical child is the harder work of the two.

4 September

Unwanted Gifts

From *The Poet at the Breakfast Table, 1872* |

Oliver Wendell Holmes (1809–1894)

– What do you do when you receive a book you don't want, from the author? – said I.

– Give him a good-natured adjective or two if I can, and thank him, and tell him I am lying under a sense of obligation to him.

– That is as good an excuse for lying as almost any, – I said.

– Yes, but look out for the fellows that send you a copy of their book to trap you into writing a book-seller's advertisement for it. I got caught so once, and never heard the end of it and never shall hear it – He took down an elegantly bound volume, on opening which appeared a flourishing and eminently flattering dedication to himself. – There, – said he, – what could I do less than acknowledge such a compliment in polite terms, and hope and expect the book would prove successful, and so forth and so forth? Well, I get a letter every few months from some new locality where the man that made that book is covering the fences with his placards, asking me whether I wrote that letter which he keeps in stereotype and has kept so any time these dozen or fifteen years.

Opinions

From *On Reading New Books, Florence, May 1825*

William Hazlitt (1778–1830)

A new work is something in our power: we mount the bench, and sit in judgment on it; we can damn or recommend it to others at pleasure, can decry or extol it to the skies, and can give an answer to those who have not yet read it and expect an account of it and thus show our shrewdness and the independence of our taste before the world have had time to form an opinion.

. . . .

If we wait, we must take our report from others; if we make haste, we may dictate ours to them. It is not a race, then, for priority of information, but for precedence in tattling and dogmatising.

To the Dean, When in England, in 1726

Thomas Sheridan (1687–1738)

To Jonathan Swift, Dean of St Patrick's Cathedral, Dublin (1713–1745)

Lines 1–12

You will excuse me, I suppose,
For sending rhyme instead of prose.
Because hot weather makes me lazy,
To write in metre is more easy.
    While you are trudging London town,
I'm strolling Dublin up and down;
While you converse with lords and dukes,
I have their betters here, my books:
Fix'd in an elbow-chair at ease,
I choose companions as I please.
I'd rather have one single shelf
Than all my friends, except yourself;
For, after all that can be said,
Our best acquaintance are the dead.

Writing

From *Manifesto, 2021* | Bernardine Evaristo (1959–)

Writing is so much more than a technical exercise. In the past I have shed tears along with my characters when I've put them through hell or made them reflect on past traumas or remember loved ones they've lost. When I was writing *Lara*, I recall rocking myself on the floor as I tried to imagine what it was like for my slave ancestors in Brazil. When my characters suffered, I suffered with them. When a character I was attached to died, I cried. I felt their tears and I felt their joy. Writing can still be experiential for me, although not quite so intensely, or so dramatically – thank God.

Writing a novel takes stamina and an unstoppable drive, more so when you're not sure you're heading in the right direction and have to start again. Every minute, every hour, every day, every week, every month, every year spent crafting a manuscript so that it materializes into your ambition for it, requires immense dedication. For every writer who produces novels at speed, there are many more of us for whom the writing process is a lot more complicated, although not unenjoyable. When writers complain that writing is painful, I wonder why they do. Surely we do it because it's incredibly rewarding.

8 September

299

Three Hours

From *An Autobiography, 1883* | Anthony Trollope (1815–1882)

All I those I think who have lived as literary men, – working daily as literary labourers, – will agree me that three hours a day will produce as much as a man ought to write. But then, he should so have trained himself that he shall be able to work continuously during those three hours, – so have tutored his mind that it shall not be necessary for him to sit nibbling his pen, and gazing at the wall before him, till he shall have found the words with which he wants to express his ideas. It had at this time become my custom, – and it still is my custom, though of late I have become a little lenient to myself, – to write with my watch before me, and to require from myself 250 words every quarter of an hour. I have found that the 250 words have been forthcoming as regularly as my watch went. But my three hours were not devoted entirely to writing. I always began my task by reading the work of the day before, an operation which would take me half an hour, and which consisted chiefly in weighing with my ear the sound of the words and phrases. I would strongly recommend this practice to all tyros in writing. That their work should be read after it has been written is a matter of course, – that it should he read twice at least before it goes to the printers, I take to be a matter of course. But by reading what he has last written, just before he recommences his task, the writer will catch the tone and spirit of what he is then saying, and will avoid the fault of seeming to be unlike himself. This division of time allowed me to produce over ten pages of an ordinary novel volume a day, and if kept up through ten months, would have given as its results three novels of three volumes each in the year; – the precise amount which so greatly acerbated the publisher in Paternoster Row, and which must at any rate be felt to be quite as much as the novel-readers of the world can want from the hands of one man.

Anthony Trollope: A System

From *Partial Portraits, 1888* | Henry James (1843–1916)

When, a few months ago, Anthony Trollope laid down his pen for the last time, it was a sign of the complete extinction of that group of admirable writers who, in England, during the preceding half century, had done so much to elevate the art of the novelist. The author of *The Warden*, of *Barchester Towers*, of *Framley Parsonage*, does not, to our mind, stand on the very same level as Dickens, Thackeray and George Eliot; for his talent was of a quality less fine than theirs. But he belonged to the same family – he had as much to tell us about English life; he was strong, genial and abundant. He published too much; the writing of novels had ended by becoming, with him, a perceptibly mechanical process.

. . . .

Trollope's fertility was gross, importunate; he himself contended, we believe, that he had given to the world a greater number of printed pages of fiction than any of his literary contemporaries. Not only did his novels follow each other without visible intermission, overlapping and treading on each other's heels, but most of these works are of extraordinary length. *Orley Farm*, *Can You Forgive Her?*, *He Knew He Was Right*, are exceedingly voluminous tales. *The Way We Live Now* is one of the longest of modern novels. Trollope produced, moreover, in the intervals of larger labour a great number of short stories, many of them charming, as well as various books of travel, and two or three biographies.

. . . .

Trollope's pace was brisker even than that of the wonderful Madame Sand and the delightful Mrs Oliphant. He had taught himself to keep this pace, and had reduced his admirable faculty to a system. Every day of his life he wrote a certain number of pages of his current tale, a number sacramental and invariable, independent of mood and place.

301

Detective Stories

From *The Sign of Four, 1890* | Arthur Conan Doyle (1859–1930)

[Sherlock Holmes on reading Dr Watson's *A Study in Scarlet*.]

'I glanced over it,' said he. 'Honestly I cannot congratulate you upon it. Detection is, or ought to be, an exact science, and should be treated in the same cold and unemotional manner. You have attempted to tinge it with romanticism, which produces much the same effect as if you worked a love-story or an elopement into the fifth proposition of Euclid.'

'But the romance was there,' I remonstrated. 'I could not tamper with the facts.'

'Some facts should be suppressed, or, at least, a just sense of proportion should be observed in treating them. The only point in the case which deserved mention was the curious analytical reasoning from effects to causes, by which I succeeded in unravelling it.'

Shop Windows

From *Riceyman Steps, 1923* | Arnold Bennett (1867–1931)

The shop had one window in King's Cross Road, but the entrance, with another window, was in Riceyman Steps. The King's Cross Road window held only cheap editions, in their paper jackets, of popular modern novels, such as those of Ethel M. Dell, Charles Garvice, Zane Grey, Florence Barclay, Nat Gould, and Gene Stratton Porter. The side window was set out with old books, first editions, illustrated editions, and complete library editions in calf or morocco of renowned and serious writers, whose works, indispensable to the collections of self-respecting book-gentlemen (as distinguished from bookmen), have passed through decades of criticism into the impregnable paradise of eternal esteem. The side window was bound to attract the attention of collectors and bibliomaniacs.

Happiness in a Bookshop

From *Martin Chuzzlewit, 1842–1844* | Charles Dickens (1812–1870)

[The bookshops] whence a pleasant smell of paper freshly pressed came issuing forth, awakening instant recollections of some new grammar had at school, long time ago, with 'Master Pinch, Grove House Academy,' inscribed in faultless writing on the fly-leaf! That whiff of russia leather, too, and all those rows on rows of volumes neatly ranged within – what happiness did they suggest! And in the window were the spick-and-span new works from London, with the title-pages, and sometimes even the first page of the first chapter, laid wide open; tempting unwary men to begin to read the book, and then, in the impossibility of turning over, to rush blindly in, and buy it! Here too were the dainty frontispiece and trim vignette, pointing like handposts on the outskirts of great cities, to the rich stock of incident beyond; and store of books, with many a grave portrait and time-honoured name, whose matter he knew well, and would have given mines to have, in any form, upon the narrow shell beside his bed at Mr Pecksniff's. What a heart-breaking shop it was!

A Personal Collection

From *The Antiquary, 1816* | Sir Walter Scott (1771–1832)

The collection was, indeed, a curious one, and might well be envied
by an amateur. Yet it was not collected at the enormous prices
of modern times, which are sufficient to have appalled the most
determined as well as earliest bibliomaniac upon record, whom
we take to have been none else than the renowned Don Quixote
de la Mancha, as, among other slight indications of an infirm
understanding, he is stated, by his veracious historian, Cid Hamet
Benengeli, to have exchanged fields and farms for folios and quartos
of chivalry. In this species of exploit, the good knight-errant has been
imitated by lords, knights, and squires of our own day, though we
have not yet heard of any that has mistaken an inn for a castle, or
laid his lance in rest against a windmill. Mr Oldbuck did not follow
these collectors in such excess of expenditure; but taking a pleasure
in the personal labour of forming his library, saved his purse at the
expense of his time and toil.

Placing Your Books

From *The Private Library, 1897* | A. L. Humphreys (1865–1946)

Junior Assistant and later Partner, Hatchards Bookshop (1881–1924)

In planning out how your books are to be placed, a great
consideration is the placing of them, so that books likely to be
frequently referred to shall be easy of access, and books less likely to
be in request shall be housed higher up. (1) Reference books should,
as far as possible, be placed together, and all easy of access. The main
divisions into which a private library classes itself are History and
Biography, Fiction, Poetry and Drama, Theology, Travel, Art, Belles
lettres; but there are so many considerations besides those of subject
in any general classification which should determine the position of
a volume that I must emphasise what has already been said about
actual personal convenience being first studied, and the library as
arranged on the shelves should be the result of personal convenience
and graceful effect. This is more particularly necessary when a library
is in course of expansion. The subjects which will expand quickest,
and the space they will require, can never be accurately gauged, and
frequent upheavals and readjustments will be necessary if any rigid
plan is aimed at.

(1) No bookshelves ought to be beyond the reach of a moderately tall
person.

The Outside of a Book

From *Crotchet Castle, 1831* | Thomas Love Peacock (1785–1866)

The library of Crotchet Castle was a large and well furnished apartment, opening on one side into an anteroom, on the other into a music-room. It had several tables stationed at convenient distances; one consecrated to the novelties of literature, another to the novelties of embellishment; others unoccupied, and at the disposal of the company. The walls were covered with a copious collection of ancient and modern books; the ancient having been selected and arranged by the Reverend Doctor Folliott.

. . . .

Mr Crotchet

To be looked at: the reason for most things in a gentleman's house being in it at all; from the paper on the walls, and the drapery of the curtains even to the books in the library, of which the most essential part is the appearance of the back.

The Rev Dr Folliott

Very true, sir. As great philosophers hold that the *esse* of things is *percipi*, so a gentleman's furniture exists to be looked at. Nevertheless, sir, there are some things more fit to be looked at than others; for instance, there is nothing more fit to be looked at than the outside of a book. It is, as I may say, from repeated experience, a pure and unmixed pleasure to have a goodly volume lying before you, and to know that you may open it if you please, and need not open it unless you please. It is a resource against *ennui*, if *ennui* should come upon you. To have the resource and not to feel the *ennui*, to enjoy your bottle in the present, and your book in the indefinite future, is a delightful condition of human existence. There is no place, in which a man can move or sit, in which the outside of a book can be otherwise than an innocent and becoming spectacle. Touching this matter, there cannot, I think, be two opinions.

Scotland

From *The World of Books, 1832* | Leigh Hunt (1784–1859)

To the Editor of *Tait's Edinburgh Magazine*
The globe we inhabit is divisible into two worlds; one hardly less
tangible, and far more known than the other, – the common
geographical world, and the world of books; and the latter may
be as geographically set forth.

. . . .

We should have the border, with its banditti, towns, and woods;
Tweed-side, Melrose, and Roslin, 'Edina', otherwise called
Edinburgh and Auld Reekie, or the town of Hume, Robertson, and
others; Woodhouselee, and other classical and haunted places; the
bower built by the fair hands of 'Bessie Bell' and 'Mary Gray'; the
farm-houses of Burns's friends; the scenes of his loves and sorrows;
the land of 'Old Mortality', of the 'Gentle Shepherd' and of 'Ossian'.
The Highlands, and the great blue billowy domains of heather,
would be distinctly marked out, in their most poetical regions; and
we should have the tracks of Ben Jonson to Hawthornden, of 'Rob
Roy' to his hiding-places, and of 'Jeanie Deans' towards England.

Abbotsford, be sure, would not be left out; nor the house of the 'Antiquary', – almost as real a man as his author.

· · · · · · · · · ·

This is the Scotland of books, and a beautiful place it is. I will venture to affirm, sir, even to yourself; that it is a more beautiful place than the other Scotland, always excepting to an exile or a rover; for the former is piqued to prefer what he must not touch; and to the latter, no spot is so charming as the ugliest place that contains his beauty. Not that Scotland has not many places literally as well as poetically beautiful: I know that well enough. But you see that young man there, turning down the corner of the dullest spot in Edinburgh, with a dead wall over against it, and delight in his eyes? He sees No. 4, the house where the girl lives he is in love with. Now what that place is to him, all places are, in their proportion, to the lover of books, for he has beheld therein by the light of imagination and sympathy.

17 September

Robert Burns: Lowland and Highland

From *A Literary Pilgrim in England, 1917*

Edward Thomas (1878–1917)

Burns's country was the Western Lowlands of Scotland. Burns was the Lowlands of Scotland.

The poor, free peasantry culminated in him. Poetry does not sum up, but his poetry was the flower and the essence of that country and its peasantry. He was great because they were all at his back, their life and their literature. To speak of his country is merely to consider a few scatterings of the elements which he mixed into lasting songs. A clay cottage at Alloway, near Ayr, was his birthplace. His father held seven acres there, and built the house. While Burns was still a small schoolboy they took a larger farm near-by, and at fifteen he began to work on the poorest land in Ayrshire as his father's chief servant.

. . . .

His poetry shows us the delicate wild country at the edge of the ploughland or in the midst of it, which is the more delicate for the contrast, and perhaps for the fact that the poet had so long known the plough.

. . . .

How much he loved the Highland, 'where savage streams tumble over savage mountains, thinly overspread with savage flocks, which sparingly support as savage inhabitants,' is not quite plain. I think that he as an individual inclined to love the mountains, but that his ancestry mixed a kind of fear or hate with his love.

The Book-worms

Robert Burns (1759–1796)

Through and through the inspired leaves,
    Ye maggots, make your windings;
But, oh! respect his lordship's taste,
      And spare his golden bindings.

The Bookworm

From *The Enemies of Books, 1880* | William Blades (1824–1890)

A most destructive Enemy of books has been the bookworm. I say 'has been,' because, fortunately, his ravages in all civilised countries have been greatly restricted during the last fifty years. This is due partly to the increased reverence for antiquity which has been universally developed – more still to the feeling of cupidity, which has caused all owners to take care of volumes which year by year have become more valuable – and, to some considerable extent, to the falling off in the production of *edible* books.

The monks, who were the chief makers as well as the custodians of books, through the long ages we call 'dark,' because so little is known of them, had no fear of the bookworm before their eyes, for, ravenous as he is and was, he loves not parchment, and at that time paper was not. Whether at a still earlier period he attacked the papyrus, the paper of the Egyptians, I know not – probably he did, as it was a purely vegetable substance; and if so, it is quite possible that the worm of to-day, in such evil repute with us, is the lineal descendant of ravenous ancestors who plagued the sacred Priests of On in the time of Joseph's Pharaoh, by destroying their title deeds and their books of Science.

Rare things and precious, as manuscripts were before the invention of typography, are well preserved, but when the printing-press was invented and paper books were multiplied in the earth; when libraries increased and readers were many, then familiarity bred contempt; books were packed in out-of-the-way places and neglected, and the oft-quoted, though seldom seen, bookworm became an acknowledged tenant of the library, and the mortal enemy of the bibliophile.

20 September

312

Learning and Reading

From *Hours in a Library* | Virginia Woolf (1882–1941)

Times Literary Supplement, 30th November, 1916

Let us begin by clearing up the old confusion between the man who loves learning and the man who loves reading, and point out that there is no connexion whatever between the two. A learned man is a sedentary, concentrated, solitary enthusiast, who searches through books to discover some particular grain of truth upon which he has set his heart. If the passion for reading conquers him, his gains dwindle and vanish between his fingers. A reader, on the other hand, must check the desire for learning at the outset; if knowledge sticks to him well and good, but to go in pursuit of it, to read on a system, to become a specialist or an authority, is very apt to kill what it suits us to consider the more humane passion for pure and disinterested reading.

Reading and Writing

From *Great Expectations, 1861* | Charles Dickens (1812–1870)

Much of my unassisted self, and more by the help of Biddy than of Mr Wopsle's great-aunt, I struggled through the alphabet as if it had been a bramble-bush; getting considerably worried and scratched by every letter. After that, I fell among those thieves, the nine figures, who seemed every evening to do something new to disguise themselves and baffle recognition. But, at last I began, in a purblind groping way, to read, write, and cipher, on the very smallest scale.

One night I was sitting in the chimney corner with my slate, expending great efforts on the production of a letter to Joe. I think it must have been a full year after our hunt upon the marshes, for it was a long time after, and it was winter and a hard frost. With an alphabet on the hearth at my feet for reference, I contrived in an hour or two to print and smear this epistle:

'mI deEr JO i opE U r krWitE wEll i opE i shAl soN B haBelL 4 2 teeDge U JO aN theN wE shOrl b sO glOdd aN wEn i M preNgtD 2 u JO woT larX an blEvE ME inF xn PiP.'

There was no indispensable necessity for my communicating with Joe by letter, inasmuch as he sat beside me and we were alone. But I delivered this written communication (slate and all) with my own hand, and Joe received it as a miracle of erudition.

'I say, Pip, old chap!' cried Joe, opening his blue eyes wide, 'what a scholar you are! Ain't you?'

'I should like to be,' said I, glancing at the slate as he held it; with a misgiving that the writing was rather hilly.

'Why, here's a J,' said Joe, 'and a O equal to anythink! Here's a J and a O, Pip, and a J-O, Joe.'

I had never heard Joe read aloud to any greater extent than this monosyllable, and I had observed at church last Sunday, when I accidentally held our Prayer-Book upside down, that it seemed to suit his convenience quite as well as if it had been all right. Wishing to embrace the present occasion of finding out whether in teaching Joe, I should have to begin quite at the beginning, I said, 'Ah! But read the rest, Jo.'

'The rest, eh, Pip?' said Joe, looking at it with a slow, searching eye, 'One, two, three. Why, here's three Js, and three Os, and three J-O, Joes in it, Pip!'

I leaned over Joe, and, with the aid of my forefinger read him the whole letter.

'Astonishing!' said Joe, when I had finished. 'You ARE a scholar.'

'How do you spell Gargery, Joe?' I asked him, with a modest patronage.

'I don't spell it at all,' said Joe.

'But supposing you did?'

'It *can't* be supposed,' said Joe. 'Tho' I'm uncommon fond of reading, too.'

'Are you, Joe?'

'On-common. Give me,' said Joe, 'a good book, or a good newspaper, and sit me down afore a good fire, and I ask no better. Lord!' he continued, after rubbing his knees a little, 'when you *do* come to a J and a O, and says you, "Here, at last, is a J-O, Joe," how interesting reading is!'

I derived from this, that Joe's education, like Steam, was yet in its infancy.

Forbidden to Read

From *Twelve Years a Slave, 1854* | Solomon Northup (1807/8–c. 1863)

Soon after he purchased me, Epps asked me if I could write and read, and on being informed that I had received some instruction in those branches of education, he assured me, with emphasis, if he ever caught me with a book, or with pen and ink, he would give me a hundred lashes. He said he wanted me to understand that he bought 'niggers' to work and not to educate.

23 September

The Lasting Mansions of the Dead

From *The Library, 1808* | George Crabbe (1754–1832)

With awe, around these silent walks I tread;
These are the lasting mansions of the dead:–
'The dead!' methinks a thousand tongues reply;
'These are the tombs of such as cannot die!'
Crown'd with eternal fame, they sit sublime,
'And laugh at all the little strife of time.'
    Hail, then, immortals! ye who shine above,
Each, in his sphere, the literary Jove;
And ye the common people of these skies,
A humbler crowd of nameless deities;
Whether 'tis yours to lead the willing mind
Through History's mazes, and the turnings find;
Or, whether led by Science, ye retire,
Lost and bewilder'd in the vast desire;
Whether the Muse invites you to her bowers,
And crowns your placid brows with living flowers;
Or godlike Wisdom teaches you to show
The noblest road to happiness below;
Or men and manners prompt the easy page
To mark the flying follies of the age:
Whatever good ye boast, that good impart;
Inform the head and rectify the heart.

The British Museum

From *On Books and the Housing of Them, 1890*

W. E. Gladstone (1809–1898)

The British Museum had only reached 115,000 when Panizzi became keeper in 1837. Nineteen years afterwards he left it with 560,000, a number which must now have more than doubled. By his noble design for occupying the central quadrangle, a desert of gravel until his time, he provided additional room for 1,200,000 volumes. All this apparently enormous space for development is being eaten up with fearful rapidity; and such is the greed of the splendid library that it opens its jaws like Hades, and threatens shortly to expel the antiquities from the building, and appropriate the spaces they adorn.

Delivery of Copies to British Museum and Other Libraries

The Copyright Act, 1911: 15, 1–4

The Delivery of Books to Libraries

(1) The publisher of every book published in the United Kingdom shall, within one month after the publication, deliver, at his own expense, a copy of the book to the trustees of the British Museum, who shall give a written receipt for it.

(2) He shall also, if written demand is made before the expiration of twelve months after publication, deliver within one month after receipt of that written demand or, if the demand was made before publication, within one month after publication, to some depot in London named in the demand a copy of the book for, or in accordance with the directions of, the authority having the control of each of the following libraries, namely: the Bodleian Library, Oxford, the University Library, Cambridge, the Library of the Faculty of Advocates at Edinburgh, and the Library of Trinity College, Dublin, and subject to the provisions of this section the National Library of Wales. In the case of an encyclopaedia, newspaper, review, magazine, or work published in a series of numbers or parts, the written demand may include all numbers or parts of the work which may be subsequently published.

(3) The copy delivered to the trustees of the British Museum shall be a copy of the whole book with all maps and illustrations belonging thereto, finished and coloured in the same manner as the best copies of the book are published, and shall be bound, sewed, or stitched together, and on the best paper on which the book is printed.

(4) The copy delivered for the other authorities mentioned in this section shall be on the paper on which the largest number of copies of the book is printed for sale, and shall be in the like condition as the books prepared for sale.

The End of the Book?

From *The British Library and the St Pancras Building, 1994*

Sir Anthony Kenny (1931–)

None of the current indications suggest the prognosis that the book as we know it is suffering from any terminal illness. Certainly, more and more information, of the kind previously accessible only on printed paper, is becoming available in electronic form, whether online or on CD-ROM. But there is no evidence that this is leading to any reduction in the demand for books. If anything, book production seems to be increasing. In 1990–1991 fifty-four thousand monographs were received on legal deposit as the British Library; in 1993–1994 the figure was seventy-two thousand.*

Let us waive this and grant, wildly unlikely as it is, that by the year two thousand hardcopy monographs are no longer published and that all journals appear only in electronic form. Even so, it cannot be supposed that the human race will lose all interest in its intellectual history prior to the electronic age. There will still be readers who will want access to the volumes now held by the British Library for reading in Bloomsbury. The new library at St Pancras will provide the appropriate environment for these to be preserved and consulted. This alone would justify its construction, even if no new books were ever to be added to its collection.

* Just over ten years later the UK produced over 200,000 new titles (Martyn Lyons, *Books: A Living History*, Thames and Hudson, 2011).

A Precious Treasure

From *The Prelude, 1850* | William Wordsworth (1770-1850)

Book Fifth: Books, lines 460–490

A precious treasure had I long possessed,
A little yellow, canvas-covered book,
A slender abstract of the Arabian tales;
And, from companions in a new abode,
When first I learnt, that this dear prize of mine
Was but a block hewn from a mighty quarry –
That there were four large volumes, laden all
With kindred matter, 'twas to me, in truth,
A promise scarcely earthly. Instantly,
With one not richer than myself, I made
A covenant that each should lay aside
The moneys he possessed, and hoard up more,
Till our joint savings had amassed enough
To make this book our own. Through several months,
In spite of all temptation, we preserved
Religiously that vow; but firmness failed,
Nor were we ever masters of our wish.

And when thereafter to my father's house
The holidays returned me, there to find
That golden store of books which I had left,
What joy was mine! How often in the course
Of those glad respites, though a soft west wind
Ruffled the waters to the angler's wish,
For a whole day together, have I lain
Down by thy side, O Derwent! murmuring stream,
On the hot stones, and in the glaring sun,
And there have read, devouring as I read,
Defrauding the day's glory, desperate!
Till with a sudden bound of smart reproach,
Such as an idler deals with in his shame,
I to the sport betook myself again.

George Eliot: A Poor View of Novels

From *Partial Portraits, 1888* | Henry James (1843–1916)

It was not till Marian Evans was past thirty, indeed, that she became an author by profession, and it may accordingly be supposed that her early letters are those which take us most into her confidence. This is true of those written when she was on the threshold of womanhood, which form a very full expression of her feelings at the time. The drawback here is that the feelings themselves are rather wanting in interest – one may almost say in amiability. At the age of twenty Marian Evans was a deeply religious young woman, whose faith took the form of a narrow evangelicism. Religious, in a manner, she remained to the end of her life, in spite of her adoption of a scientific explanation of things; but in the year 1839 she thought it ungodly to go to concerts and to read novels.

. . . .

This was only a moment in her development; but there is something touching in the contrast between such a state of mind and that of the woman before whom, at middle age, all the culture of the world unrolled itself, and towards whom fame and fortune, and an activity which at the earlier period she would have thought very profane, pressed with rapidity. In 1839, as I have said, she thought very meanly of the art in which she was to attain such distinction. 'I venture to believe that the same causes which exist in my own breast to render novels and romances pernicious have their counterpart in every fellow-creature … The weapons of Christian warfare were never sharpened at the forge of romance.'

Story Telling

From *Middlemarch, 1871-1872* | George Eliot (1819–1880)

Mrs Vincy: 'But my children are all good-tempered, thank God.'

This was easily credible to any one looking at Mrs Vincy as she threw back her broad cap-strings, and smiled towards her three little girls, aged from seven to eleven. But in that smiling glance she was obliged to include Mary Garth, whom the three girls had got into a corner to make her tell them stories. Mary was just finishing the delicious tale of Rumpelstiltskin, which she had well by heart, because Letty was never tired of communicating it to her ignorant elders from a favourite red volume. Louisa, Mrs Vincy's darling, now ran to her with wide-eyed serious excitement, crying, 'O mamma, mamma, the little man stamped so hard on the floor he couldn't got his leg out again!'

'Bless you, my cherub!' said mamma; 'you shall tell me all about it to-morrow. Go and listen!' and then, as her eyes followed Louisa back towards the attractive corner, she thought that if Fred wished her to invite Mary again she would make no objection, the children being so pleased with her.

But presently the corner became still more animated, for Mr Farebrother came in, and seating himself behind Louisa, took her on his lap; whereupon the girls all insisted that he must hear Rumpelstiltskin, and Mary must tell it over again. He insisted too, and Mary, without fuss, began again in her neat fashion, with precisely the same words as before. Fred, who had also seated himself near, would have felt unmixed triumph in Mary's effectiveness if Mr Farebrother had not been looking at her with evident admiration, while he dramatised an intense interest in the tale to please the children.

OCTOBER

The Art of Bookbinding

Women Novelists

From *The Victorian Age in Literature, 1913*

G. K. Chesterton (1874–1936)

The women have, on the whole, equality; and certainly, in some points, superiority. Jane Austen is as strong in her own way as Scott is in his. But she is, for all practical purposes, never weak in her own way – and Scott very often is. Charlotte Brontë dedicated *Jane Eyre* to the author of *Vanity Fair*. I should hesitate to say that Charlotte Brontë's is a better book than Thackeray's, but I think it might well be maintained that it is a better story.

1 October

First Lines

From *Jane Eyre, 1847* | Charlotte Brontë (1816–1855)

There was no possibility of taking a walk that day. We had been wandering, indeed, in the leafless shrubbery an hour in the morning; but since dinner (Mrs Reed, when there was no company, dined early) the cold winter wind had brought with it clouds so sombre and a rain so penetrating, that further outdoor exercise was now out of the question.

I was glad of it: I never liked long walks, especially on chilly afternoons: dreadful to me was the coming home in the raw twilight, with nipped fingers and toes, and a heart saddened by the chidings of Bessie, the nurse, and humbled by the consciousness of my physical inferiority to Eliza, John, and Georgiana Reed.

The said Eliza, John, and Georgiana were now clustered round their mamma in the drawing-room: she lay reclined on a sofa by the fireside, and with her darlings about her (for the time neither quarrelling nor crying) looked perfectly happy. Me, she had dispensed from joining the group; saying, 'She regretted to be under the necessity of keeping me at a distance; but that until she heard from Bessie and could discover by her own observation that I was endeavouring in good earnest to acquire a more sociable and child-like disposition, a more attractive and sprightly manner – something lighter, franker, more natural, as it were – she really must exclude me from privileges intended only for contented, happy little children.'

The Preface

From *Dictionary of Phrase and Fable, 1870* |

Rev. Ebenezer Cobham Brewer (1810–1897)

'What has this babbler to say?' is substantially the question of every one to whom a new book is offered. For ourselves, it will be difficult to furnish an answer in a sentence equally terse and explicit; yet our book has a definite scope and distinct speciality, which we will proceed to unfold. We call it a 'Dictionary of Phrase and Fable,' a title wide enough, no doubt, to satisfy a very lofty ambition, yet not sufficiently wide to describe the miscellaneous contents of this 'alms-basket of words.' As the Gargantuan course of studies included everything known to man and something more, so this sweep-net of a book encloses anything that comes within its reach. It draws incurious or novel etymologies, pseudonyms and popular titles, local traditions and literary blunders, biographical and historical trifles too insignificant to find a place in books of higher pretension, but not too worthless to be worth knowing. Sometimes a criticism is adventured, sometimes an exposition. Vulgar errors, of course, form an item; for the prescience of the ant in laying up a store for winter, the wisdom of the bee in the peculiar shape of its honey-comb, the disinterestedness of the jackal, the poisonous nature of the upas tree, and the striding of the Rhodian Colossos, if not of the nature of fable, are certainly 'more strange than true.'

The Bibliomaniac's Prayer

Eugene Field (1850–1895)

Keep me, I pray, in wisdom's way
    That I may truths eternal seek;
I need protecting care to-day, –
    My purse is light, my flesh is weak.
So banish from my erring heart
    All baleful appetites and hints
Of Satan's fascinating art,
    Of first editions, and of prints.
Direct me in some godly walk
    Which leads away from bookish strife,
That I with pious deed and talk
    May extra-illustrate my life.

But if, O Lord, it pleaseth Thee
    To keep me in temptation's way,
I humbly ask that I may be
    Most notably beset to-day;
Let my temptation be a book,
    Which I shall purchase, hold, and keep,
Whereon when other men shall look,
    They'll wail to know I got it cheap.
Oh, let it such a volume be
    As in rare copperplates abounds,
Large paper, clean, and fair to see,
    Uncut, unique, unknown to Lowndes.

The Opening Letter

From *84 Charing Cross Road, 1971* | Helene Hanff (1916–1997)

14 East 95th St

New York City
October 5, 1949

Marks & Co.
84, Charing Cross Road
London, W.C.2
England

Gentleman:

Your ad in the *Saturday Review of Literature* says that you specialize in out-of-print books. The phrase 'antiquarian book-sellers' scares me somewhat, as I equate 'antique' with expensive. I am a poor writer with an antiquarian taste in books and all the things I want are impossible to get over here except in very expensive rare editions, or in Barnes & Noble's grimy, marked-up school-boy copies.

I enclose a list of my most pressing problems. If you have clean secondhand copies of any of the books on the list for no more than $5.00 each, will you consider this a purchase order and send them to me?

Very truly yours,
Helene Hanff
(Miss) Helene Hanff

5 October

George Crabbe

From *Diary, 1874* | Francis Kilvert (1840–1879)

This month there is in the *Cornhill Magazine* an article on Crabbe's
poetry. My Father says he remembers staying with the Longmires
at Wingfield about the year 1830. They took him one afternoon to
a book sale at Trowbridge, of which parish the poet Crabbe was
then Rector. In the evening the whole party adjourned to the rectory,
where they found Crabbe playing whist with three friends in a
large drawing room. Crabbe's son (who was acting as his father's
curate) was present, a keen-looking laughable man, an exaggerated
likeness of Henry Dew. He came forward to receive the visitors while
Crabbe continued his game. My Father describes the poet as being
a small insignificant-looking old man, bald and with a whitish
yellow complexion.

Books

From *The Library*, 1808 | George Crabbe (1754–1832)

But what strange art, what magic can dispose
The troubled mind to change its native woes?
Or lead us willing from ourselves, to see
Others more wretched, more undone than we?
This BOOKS can do; – nor this alone; they give
New views to life, and teach us how to live;
They soothe the grieved, the stubborn they chastise,
Fools they admonish, and confirm the wise:
Their aid they yield to all: they never shun
The man of sorrow, nor the wretch undone:
Unlike the hard, the selfish, and the proud,
They fly not sullen from the suppliant crowd;
Nor tell to various people various things,
But show to subjects what they show to kings.

Reading Shakespeare Aloud

From *Mansfield Park, 1714* | Jane Austen (1775–1817)

[Fanny Price is reading Shakespeare to Lady Bertram when Edward Bertram and Henry Crawford walk into the drawing room.]

Crawford took the volume. 'Let me have the pleasure of finishing that speech to your ladyship,' said he. 'I shall find it immediately.' And by carefully giving way to the inclination of the leaves, he did find it, or within a page or two, quite near enough to satisfy Lady Bertram, who assured him, as soon as he mentioned the name of Cardinal Wolsey, that he had got the very speech – Not a look, or an offer of help had Fanny given; not a syllable for or against. All her attention was for her work. She seemed determined to be interested by nothing else. But taste was too strong in her. She could not abstract her mind five minutes; she was forced to listen; his reading was capital, and her pleasure in good reading extreme. To good reading, however, she had been long used; her uncle read well – her cousins all – Edmund very well; but in Mr. Crawford's reading there was a variety of excellence beyond what she had ever met with. The King, the Queen, Buckingham, Wolsey, Cromwell, all were given in turn; for with the happiest knack, the happiest power of jumping and guessing, he could always light, at will, on the best scene, or the best speeches of each; and whether it were dignity or pride, or tenderness or remorse, or whatever were to be expressed, he could do it with equal beauty. – It was truly dramatic. – His acting had first taught Fanny what pleasure a play might give, and his reading brought all his acting before her again; nay, perhaps with greater enjoyment, for it came unexpectedly, and with no such drawback as she had been used to suffer in seeing him on the stage with Miss Bertram.

Reading Aloud

From *I Know Why the Caged Bird Sings*, 1969

Maya Angelou (1928–2014)

9 October

'Come and walk along with me, Marguerite.' I couldn't have refused even if I'd wanted to. She pronounced my name so nicely. Or more correctly, she spoke each word with such clarity that I was certain a foreigner who didn't understand English could have understood her.

'Now no one is going to make you talk – possibly no one can. But bear in mind, language is man's way of communicating with his fellow man and it is language alone which separates him from the lower animals.' That was a totally new idea to me, and I would need time to think about it,

'Your grandmother says you read a lot. Every chance you get. That's good, but not good enough. Words mean more than what is set down on paper. It takes the human voice to infuse them with shades of deeper meaning.'

I memorized the part about the human voice infusing words. It seemed so valid and poetic.

She said she was going to give me some books and that I not only must read them, I must read them aloud. She suggested I try to make a sentence sound in as many different ways as possible.

Reading Kipling Aloud

From *The English Patient, 1992* | Michael Ondaatje (1943–)

Novels commenced with hesitation or chaos. Readers were never fully in balance. A door a lock a weir opened and they rushed through, one hand holding a gunnel, the other a hat.

When she begins a book she enters through stilted doorways into large courtyards. Parma and Paris and India spread their carpets.

He sat, in defiance of municipal orders, astride the gun Zam-zammah on her brick platform opposite the old Ajaib-Gher – the Wonder House, as the natives called the Lahore Museum. Who hold Zam-zammah, that 'fire-breathing dragon,' hold the Punjab; for the great green-bronze piece is always first of the conqueror's loot.

'Read him slowly, dear girl, you must read Kipling slowly. Watch carefully where the commas fall so you can discover the natural pauses. He is a writer who used pen and ink. He looked up from the page a lot, I believe, stared through his window and listened to the birds, as most writers who are alone do. Some do not know the names of the birds, though he did. Your eye is too quick and North American. Think about the spread of his pen. What an appalling, barnacled old first paragraph it is otherwise.

Confusion

From *Remembrance of Things Past: Swann's Way, 1922*

Marcel Proust (1871–1922)

Published in France, *Du côté de chez Swann*, 1913

Overture

Mamma sat down by my bed; she had chosen *François le Champi*, whose reddish cover and incomprehensible title gave it a distinct personality in my eyes and a mysterious attraction. I had not then read any real novels. I had heard it said that George Sand was a typical novelist. That prepared me in advance to imagine that *François le Champi* contained something inexpressibly delicious. The course of the narrative, where it tended to arouse curiosity or melt to pity, certain modes of expression which disturb or sadden the reader, and which, with a little experience, he may recognise as 'common form' in novels, seemed to me then distinctive – for to me a new book was not one of a number of similar objects, but was like an individual man, unmatched, and with no cause of existence beyond himself – an intoxicating whiff of the peculiar essence of *François le Champi*. Beneath the everyday incidents, the commonplace thoughts and hackneyed words, I could hear, or overhear, an intonation, a rhythmic utterance fine and strange. The 'action' began: to me it seemed all the more obscure because in those days, when I read to myself, I used often, while I turned the pages, to dream of something quite different. And to the gaps which this habit made in my knowledge of the story more were added by the fact that when it was Mamma who was reading to me aloud she left all the love-scenes out. And so all the odd changes which take place in the relations between the Miller's wife and the boy, changes which only the birth and growth of love can explain, seemed to me plunged and steeped in a mystery, the key to which (as I could readily believe) lay in that strange and pleasant-sounding name of *Champi*, which draped the boy who wore it, I know not why, in its own bright colour, purpurate and charming.

Knowing One's Books

From *Gossip in a Library, 1891* | Edmund Gosse (1849–1928)

To possess few books, and those not too rich and rare for daily use, has this advantage, that the possessor can make himself master of them all, can recollect their peculiarities, and often remind himself of their contents. The man that has two or three thousand books can be familiar with them all; he that has thirty thousand can hardly have a speaking acquaintance with more than a few.

12 October

The Scent of a Book

From *The Private Papers of Henry Ryecroft, 1903*

George Gissing (1857–1903)

I know every book of mine by its *scent*, and I have but to put my nose between the pages to be reminded of all sorts of things. My Gibbon, for example, my well-bound eight-volume Milman edition, which I have read and read and read again for more than thirty years – never do I open it but the scent of the noble page restores to me all the exultant happiness of that moment when I received it as a prize.

Or my Shakespeare, the great Cambridge Shakespeare – it has an odour which carries me yet farther back in life; for these volumes belonged to my father, and before I was old enough to read them with understanding, it was often permitted me, as a treat, to take down one of them from the bookcase, and reverently to turn the leaves. The volumes smell exactly as they did in that old time, and what a strange tenderness comes upon me when I hold one of them in hand.

Why Fiction is Valuable

From *Dæmon Voices: Balloon Debate, 2002* | Philip Pullman (1946–)

Novels and stories are not arguments; they set out not to convince, but to beguile. When you write a story you're not trying to prove anything or demonstrate the merits of this case or the flaws in that. At its simplest, what you're doing is making up some interesting events, putting them in the best order to show the connections between them, and recounting them as clearly as you can; and your intention is to make the audience sufficiently delighted or moved to buy your next book when it comes out in due course.

. . . .

Most of all, stories give *delight*. That's the point I began with, and I'll come back to it to finish up: they b*eguile*. They bewitch, they enchant, they cast a spell, they enthral; they hold children from their play, and old men from the chimney corner.

Hamlet, Don Quixote, Mr Pickwick and Others

From *Note-books, 1912* | Samuel Butler (1835–1902)

The great characters of fiction live as truly as the memories of dead men. For the life after death it is not necessary that a man or woman should have lived.

A Discerning and Unprejudiced Reader

From *Northanger Abbey, 1817* | Jane Austen (1775–1817)

'Have you ever read *Udolpho*, Mr Thorpe?'

'*Udolpho!* Oh, Lord! not I; I never read novels; I have something else to do.'

Catherine, humbled and ashamed, was going to apologise for her question, but he prevented her by saying, 'Novels are all so full of nonsense and stuff; there has not been a tolerably decent one come out since *Tom Jones*, except the *Monk*, I read that t'other day, but as for all the others, they are the stupidest things in creation.

'I think you must like *Udolpho*, if you were to read it; it is so very interesting.'

'Not I faith! No, if I read any, it shall be Mrs Radcliffe's; her novels are amusing enough, they are worth reading; some fun and nature in them.'

'*Udolpho* was written by Mrs Radcliffe,' said Catherine, with some hesitation from the fear of mortifying him.

'No, sure; was it? Ay, I remember, so it was; I was thinking of that other stupid book, written by that woman they make such a fuss about, she who married the French emigrant.'

'I suppose you mean *Camilla*?'

'Yes, that's the book; such unnatural stuff, – An old man playing at see-saw; I took up the first volume once, and looked it over, but I soon found it would not do; indeed, I guessed what sort of stuff it must be before I saw it; as soon as I heard she had married an emigrant, I was sure I should never be able to get through it.'

'I have never read it.'

'You had no loss, I assure you; it is the horridest nonsense you can imagine there is nothing in the world in it but an old man's playing at see-saw and learning Latin; upon my soul, there is not.'

This critique, the justness of which was unfortunately lost on poor Catherine brought them to the door of Mrs Thorpe's lodgings, and the feelings of the discerning and unprejudiced reader of *Camilla* gave way to the feelings of the dutiful and affectionate son, as they met Mrs Thorpe.

The Revolution

From *Books and Bookmen, 1892* | Andrew Lang (1844–1912)

During the Revolution, to like well-bound books was as much as
to proclaim one an aristocrat. Condorcet might have escaped the
scaffold if he had only thrown away the neat little Horace from
the royal press, which betrayed him for no true Republican, but an
educated man. The great libraries from the chateaux of the nobles
were scattered among all the book-stalls. True sons of freedom
tore off the bindings, with their gilded crests and scutcheons.
One revolutionary writer declared, and perhaps he was not far wrong,
that the art of binding was the worst enemy of reading. He always
began his studies by breaking the backs of the volumes he was about
to attack. The art of bookbinding in these sad years took flight to
England, and was kept alive by artists robust rather than refined,
like Thompson and Roger Payne. These were evil days, when
the binder had to cut the aristocratic coat of arms out of a book
cover, and glue in a gilt cap of liberty, as in a volume in an Oxford
amateur's collection.

The Truly Cultured

From *The Complete Polysyllabic Spree, 2006* | Nick Hornby (1957–)

October 2004: Gabriel Zaid, *So Many Books*

Zaid's finest moment comes in his second paragraph, when he says that 'The truly cultured are capable of owning thousands of unread books without losing their composure or their desire for more'.

That's me! And you probably! That's us! 'Thousands of unread books'! 'Truly cultured'! Look at this month's list [of books bought]: Chekhov's letters, Amis' letters, Dylan Thomas' letters . . . What are the chances of getting through that lot? I've started on the Chekhov but the Amis and the Dylan Thomas have been put straight into their permanent home on the shelves, rather than on any sort of temporary pending pile. The Dylan Thomas I saw remaindered for fifteen quid (down from fifty) just after I'd read a terrific review of a new Thomas biography in the *New Yorker*, the Amis letters were a fiver. But as I was finding a home for them in the Arts and Lit non-fiction section (I personally find that for domestic purposes, the Trivial Pursuit system works better than Dewey), I suddenly had a little epiphany: all the books we own, both read and unread, are the fullest expression of self we have at our disposal. My music is me, too, of course – but as I really only like rock and roll and its mutations, huge chunks of me – my rarely examined operatic streak, for example – are unrepresented in my CD collection. And I don't have the wall space or the money for all the art I would want, and my house is a shabby mess, ruined by the children . . . But with each passing year, and with each whimsical purchase, our libraries become more and more able to articulate who we are, whether we read the books or not. Maybe that's not worth the thirty-odd quid I blew on those collections of letters, admittedly, but it's got to be worth something, right?

Walter Scott: Child and Boy

From *A Literary Pilgrim in England, 1917*

Edward Thomas (1878–1917)

Before he was three Scott left Edinburgh for the country of his
ancestors, and came to live at Sandy-Knowe Farm in Tweeddale.
It was thought that 'natural exertion, excited by free air and liberty'
might restore the use of his lame right leg; and he says himself that
'the impatience of a child soon inclined me to struggle with my
infirmity, and I began by degrees to stand, to walk, and to run,'
to become 'a healthy, high-spirited, and, my lameness apart,
a sturdy child.'

. . . .

While still a boy he 'entered upon the dry and barren wilderness of
forms and conveyances' with his father in Edinburgh, but at the same
time composed romances in friendly rivalry with a friend, which
were rehearsed upon their walks 'to the most solitary spots about
Arthur's Seat and Salisbury Crags.' He would walk out to breakfast
at Prestonpans, and return at evening. The Law formed a background
for a very picturesque Freedom. He had, for example, 'a dreamy way
of going much farther than he intended' when he was walking or
riding or fishing above Howgate, and he tells us how on one occasion
the beauty and the hospitality of Pennycuik House 'drowned all
recollection of home for a day or two.' When his father protested that
he was meant for a pedlar, the lad was not offended. His principal
object was to see romantic scenery and places of historic interest. The
field of Bannockburn and the landscape seen from Stirling Castle
equally attracted him.

Happiness

From *Guy Mannering, 1815* | Sir Walter Scott (1771–1832)

Dominie Sampson was occupied, body and soul, in the arrangement
of the late bishop's library, which had been sent from Liverpool by
sea, and conveyed by thirty or forty carts from the seaport at which
it was landed. Sampson's joy at beholding the ponderous contents
of these chests arranged upon the floor of the large apartment, from
whence he was to transfer them to the shelves, baffles all description.
He grinned like an ogre, swung his arms like the sails of a wind-mill,
shouted 'Prodigious' till the roof rung to his raptures. 'He had never,'
he said, 'seen so many books together, except in the College Library;'
and now his dignity and delight in being superintendent of the
collection, raised him, in his own opinion, almost to the rank of the
academical librarian, whom he had always regarded as the greatest
and happiest man on earth.

The Serious Reader

From *Jane Eyre, 1847* | Charlotte Brontë (1816–1855)

I saw a girl sitting on a stone bench near. She was bent over a book, on the perusal of which she seemed intent: from where I stood I could see the title – it was *Rasselas* – a name that struck me as strange, and consequently attractive. In turning a leaf she happened to look up, and I said to her directly:–

'Is your book interesting?' I had already formed the intention of asking her to lend it to me some day.

'I like it,' she answered after a pause of a second or two, during which she examined me.

'What is it about?' I continued. I hardly know where I found the hardihood thus to open a conversation with a stranger. The step was contrary to my nature and habits; but I think her occupations touched a chord of sympathy somewhere; for I, too, liked reading, though of a frivolous and childish kind; I could not digest or comprehend the serious or substantial.

'You may look at it,' replied the girl, offering me the book.

I did so; a brief examination convinced me that the contents were less taking than the title: *Rasselas* looked dull to my trifling taste; I saw nothing about fairies, nothing about genii; no bright variety seemed spread over the closely-printed pages. I returned it to her she received it quietly.

Four Classes of Readers

From *Seven Lectures on Shakespeare and Milton:*
The Second Lecture, 1856 | Samuel Taylor Coleridge (1772–1834)

Readers may be divided into four classes:

1. Sponges, who absorb all they read, and return it nearly in the same state, only a little dirtied.

2. Sand-glasses, who retain nothing, and are content to get through a book for the sake of getting through the time.

3. Strain-bags, who retain merely the dregs of what they read.

4. Mogul diamonds, equally rare and valuable, who profit by what they read, and enable others to profit by it also.

How to Read

From *The Private Library, 1897* | A. L. Humphreys (1865–1946)

Junior Assistant and later Partner, Hatchards Bookshop (1881–1924)

The reason why so many people who read much know so little, is because they read isolated books instead of reading one book in connexion with another. The memory is trained by association, and if you read two books in succession on one subject you know more than twice as much as if you had read one book only. A good memory is a memory which assimilates. Every one has a good memory for something. A good memory rejects and sifts, and does not accept everything offered to it like a pillar-box. Do not join reading societies, because they kill individuality. Choose your subject, and work all round it.

23 October

What One Should or Shouldn't Read

From *The Importance of Being Earnest, 1895*

Oscar Wilde (1854–1900)

ALGERNON

Oh! it is absurd to have a hard-and-fast rule about what one should read and what one shouldn't. More than half of modern culture depends on what one shouldn't read.

JACK

I am quite aware of the fact, and I don't propose to discuss modern culture. It isn't the sort of thing one should talk of in private.

The Land of Story-Books

Robert Louis Stevenson (1850–1894)

At evening, when the lamp is lit,
Around the fire my parents sit;
They sit at home and talk and sing,
And do not play at anything.

Now, with my little gun, I crawl
All in the dark along the wall,
And follow round the forest track
Away behind the sofa back.

There, in the night, where none can spy,
All in my hunter's camp I lie,
And play at books that I have read
Till it is time to go to bed.

These are the hills, these are the woods,
These are my starry solitudes;
And there the river by whose brink
The roaring lions come to drink.

I see the others far away
As if in firelit camp they lay,
And I, like to an Indian scout,
Around their party prowled about.

So, when my nurse comes in for me,
Home I return across the sea,
And go to bed with backward looks
At my dear land of Story-books.

The Victorian Age

From *Eminent Victorians: Author's Preface, 1918*

Lytton Strachey (1880–1932)

The history of the Victorian Age will never be written; we know too much about it. For ignorance is the first requisite of the historian – ignorance, which simplifies and clarifies, which selects and omits, with a placid perfection unattainable by the highest art. Concerning the Age which has just passed, our fathers and our grandfathers have poured forth and accumulated so vast a quantity of information that the industry of a Ranke would be submerged by it, and the perspicacity of a Gibbon would quail before it. It is not by the direct method of a scrupulous narration that the explorer of the past can hope to depict that singular epoch. If he is wise, he will adopt a subtler strategy. He will attack his subject in unexpected places: he will fall upon the flank, or the rear; he will shoot a sudden, revealing searchlight into obscure recesses, hitherto undivined. He will row out over that great ocean of material, and lower down into it, here and there, a little bucket, which will bring up to the light of day some characteristic specimen, from those far depths, to be examined with a careful curiosity. Guided by these considerations, I have written the ensuing studies. I have attempted, through the medium of biography, to present some Victorian visions to the modern eye. They are, in one sense, haphazard visions – that is to say, my choice of subjects has been determined by no desire to construct a system or to prove a theory, but by simple motives of convenience and of art. It has been my purpose to illustrate rather than to explain. It would have been futile to hope to tell even a précis of the truth about the Victorian age, for the shortest précis must fill innumerable volumes. But, in the lives of an ecclesiastic, an educational authority, a woman of action, and a man of adventure, I have sought to examine and elucidate certain fragments of the truth which took my fancy and lay to my hand.

A Disclaimer and a Definition

From *The Victorian Age in Literature, 1913*

G. K. Chesterton (1874–1936)

The Editors wish to explain that this book is not put forward as
an authoritative history of Victorian literature. It is a free and
personal statement of views and impressions about the significance
of Victorian literature made by Mr Chesterton at the Editors'
express invitation.

. . . .

The Victorian novel was a thing entirely Victorian; quite unique
and suited to a sort of cosiness in that country and that age. But
the novel itself, though not merely Victorian, is mainly modern.
No clearheaded person wastes his time over definitions, except where
he thinks his own definition would probably be in dispute. I merely
say, therefore, that when I say 'novel', I mean a fictitious narrative
(almost invariably, but not necessarily, in prose) of which the essential
is that the story is not told for the sake of its naked pointedness as
an anecdote, or for the sake of the irrelevant landscapes and visions
that can be caught up in it, but for the sake of some study of the
difference between human beings.

27 October

A Mere Verbal Distinction

From *Sylvie and Bruno Concluded, 1893* | Lewis Carroll (1832–1898)

The Farewell Party

'The day must come – if the world lasts long enough –' said Arthur, 'when every possible tune will have been composed – every possible pun perpetrated –' (Lady Muriel wrung her hands, like a tragedy-queen) 'and, worse than that, every possible *book* written! For the number of *words* is finite.'

'It'll make very little difference to the *authors*,' I suggested. 'Instead of saying "*what* book shall I write?" an author will ask himself "*which* book shall I write?" A mere verbal distinction!'

Found in a Book

From *Diary, 1870* | Francis Kilvert (1840–1879)

Saturday 29th October

Today I found in a book a red silk handkerchief worked with the words 'forget me not', and I am sorry to say that I have entirely forgotten who gave it to me. One of my many lovers no doubt. But which?

Tristram Shandy: A Masterpiece of Digression

From *Great English Novelists*, 1908 |

George Holbrook Jackson (1874–1948)

[It] had sounded a new note in the art of the novel, and it was a note of no little importance, because it established the principle that it was by no means necessary that a novel should be dependent upon plot. Sterne's masterpiece is a section of life, without any more obvious scheme than is to be seen in the reality: a section of life seen through a distinct and fascinating temperament. Its nine volumes appeared between the years 1760 and 1767, and they contain a whole collection of types and characters entirely new to fiction. There is no special hero of the book. Tristram, who tells the tale, never really becomes an embodied personality, he is like Wordsworth's cuckoo – a wandering voice. But such a voice as literature had never heard before. *Tristram Shandy* was not only a new type of novel, it was written in a new kind of English. It scintillates with short, bright, conversational sentences, strangely held together in a scaffolding of amazing punctuation: colons, semi-colons, commas, with the minimum of full-stops and the maximum of communicative dashes, working together with wonderful volubility – like the varying expressions on the face of a talker – in fact, Stern invented in *Tristram* a written colloquial language.

Writing, Properly Managed

From *The Life and Opinions of Tristram Shandy, 1759–1767*

Laurence Sterne (1713–1768)

Writing, when properly managed (as you may be sure I think mine is) is but a different name for conversation: As no one, who knows what he is about in good company, would venture to talk all; – so no author, who understands the just boundaries of decorum and good-breeding, would presume to think all: The truest respect which you can pay to the reader's understanding, is to halve this matter amicably, and leave him something to imagine, in his turn, as well as yourself.

For my own part, I am eternally paying him compliments of this kind, and do all that lies in my power to keep his imagination as busy as my own.

NOVEMBER

An Abundant Library

Buying a Bookshop

From *The Diary of a Bookseller, 2017* | Shaun Bythell (1970–)

When I first saw The Book Shop in Wigtown I was eighteen years
old, back in my home town and about to leave for university. I clearly
remember walking past it with a friend and commenting that I was
quite certain that it would be closed within the year. Twelve years
later, while visiting my parents at Christmas time, I called in to see
if they had a copy of *Three Fevers* in stock, by Leo Walmsley,
and while I was talking to the owner, admitted to him that I was
struggling to find a job that I enjoyed. He suggested that I buy his
shop since he was keen to retire. When I told him that I didn't have
any money, he replied, 'You don't need money – what do you think
banks are for?' Less than a year later, on 1 November 2001, a month
(to the day) after my thirty-first birthday, the place became mine.
Before I took over I ought perhaps to have read a piece of George
Orwell's writing published in 1936. 'Bookshop Memories' rings as
true today as it did then, and sounds a salutary warning to anyone
as naive as I was that the world of selling second-hand books is not
quite an idyll of sitting in an armchair by a roaring fire with your
slipper-clad feet up, smoking a pipe and reading Gibbon's *Decline and
Fall* while a stream of charming customers engages you in intelligent
conversation, before parting with fistfuls of cash. In fact, the truth
could scarcely be more different.

Booksellers

From *Dear Howard, 2018* | David Batterham (1933–)

Booksellers are often rather odd. This is not surprising since we
have all managed to escape or avoid more regular forms of work.

It is also a trade for which there are no rules. It can be conducted
from a shop in Bond Street, from a barrow or a car boot. Some
booksellers get most of their books from sales, some by clearing
houses; others, like myself, simply by buying books from other
bookseller's shops.

2 November

Customers

From *Bookshop Memories, 1936* | George Orwell (1903–1950)

When I worked in a second-hand bookshop – so easily pictured,
if you don't work in one, as a kind of paradise where charming old
gentlemen browse eternally among calf-bound folios – the thing
that chiefly struck me was the rarity of really bookish people. Our
shop had an exceptionally interesting stock, yet I doubt whether ten
per cent of our customers knew a good book from a bad one. First
edition snobs were much commoner than lovers of literature, but
oriental students haggling over cheap textbooks were commoner still,
and vague-minded women looking for birthday presents for their
nephews were commonest of all.

. . . .

In a town like London there are always plenty of not quite certifiable
lunatics walking the streets, and they tend to gravitate towards
bookshops, because a bookshop is one of the few places where you
can hang about for a long time without spending any money.

To My Booke-Seller

Ben Jonson (1572–1637)

Epigrammes II

Thou, that mak'st gaine thy end, and wisely well,
Call'st a booke good, or bad, as it doth sell,
Use mine so, too: I give thee leave. But crave
For the lucks sake, it thus much favour have,
To lye upon thy stall, till it be sought;
Not offer'd, as it made sute to be bought;
Nor have my title-leafe on posts, or walls,
Or in cleft-sticks, advanced to make calls
For termers, or some clarke-like serving-man,
Who scarse can spell th'hard names: whose knight lesse can.
If, without these vile arts, it will not sell,
Send it to Bucklers-bury, there 'twill, well.

Writing a Book on the Australasian Colonies

From *An Autobiography, 1883* | Anthony Trollope (1815–1882)

It was a better book than that which I had written eleven years before on the American States, but not so good as that on the West Indies in 1859. As regards the information given, there was much more to be said about Australia than the West Indies. Very much more is said, – and very much more may be learned from the latter than from the former book. I am sure that any one who will take the trouble to read the book on Australia, will learn much from it. But the West Indian volume was readable. I am not sure that either of the other works are, in the proper sense of that word. When I go back to them I find that the pages drag with me; – and if so with me, how must it be with others who have none of that love which a father feels even for his ill-favoured offspring. Of all the needs a book has the chief need is that it be readable.

My Father's Shakespeare

Wendy Cope (1945–)

My father must have bought it second-hand,
Inscribed 'To RS Elwyn' – who was he?
Published 1890, leather-bound,
In 1961 passed on to me.
November 6th. How old was I? Sixteen.
Doing A level in English Lit.,
In love with Keats and getting very keen
On William Shakespeare. I was thrilled with it,
This gift, glad then, as now, to think
I had been chosen as the keeper of
My father's Shakespeare, where, in dark blue ink,
He wrote, 'To Wendy Mary Cope. With love.'
Love on a page, surviving death and time.
He didn't even have to make it rhyme.

Sonnet XXIII

William Shakespeare (1564–1616)

As an unperfect actor on the stage,
Who with his fear is put besides his part,
Or some fierce thing, replete with too much rage,
Whose strength's abundance weakens his own heart;
So I, for fear of trust, forget to say
The perfect ceremony of love's right,
And in mine own love's strength seem to decay,
O'ercharged with burthen of mine own love's might.
O, let my books be then the eloquence
And dumb presagers of my speaking breast,
Who plead for love, and look for recompense,
More than that tongue that more hath more expressed:
    O learn to read what silent love hath writ!
    To hear with eyes belongs to love's fine wit.

On Shakespeare

From *An Essay of Dramatic Poesy, 1668* | John Dryden (1631–1700)

He was the man who of all modern, and perhaps ancient poets, had
the largest and most comprehensive soul. All the images of nature
were still present to him, and he drew them, not laboriously, but
luckily; when he describes any thing, you more than see it, you feel
it too. Those who accuse him to have wanted learning, give him the
greater commendation: he was naturally learned; he needed not the
spectacles of books to read nature; he looked inwards, and found
her there. I cannot say he is every where alike; were he so, I should
do him injury to compare him with the greatest of mankind. He is
many times flat, insipid; his comick wit degenerating into clenches,
his serious swelling into bombast. But he is always great, when some
great occasion is presented to him; no man can say he ever had a fit
subject for his wit, and did not then raise himself as high above the
rest of poets.

Language

From *Why be Happy When You Could Be Normal?* 2011

Jeanette Winterson (1959–)

Working-class families in the north of England used to hear the 1611 Bible regularly at church and at home and as there was still a 'thee' and 'thou' or 'tha' in daily speech for us, the language didn't seem too difficult. I especially liked 'the quick and the dead' – you really get a feel for the difference if you live in a house with mice and a mousetrap.

In the 1960s many men – and they were men not women – attended evening classes at the Working Men's Institutes or the Mechanics' Institute – another progressive initiative coming out of Manchester. The idea of 'bettering' yourself was not seen as elitist then, nor was it assumed that all values are relative, nor that all culture is more or less identical – whether Hammer Horror or Shakespeare.

Those evening classes were big on Shakespeare – and none of the men ever complained that the language was difficult. Why not? It wasn't difficult – it was the language of the 1611 Bible; the King James Version appeared in the same year as the first advertised performance of *The Tempest*. Shakespeare wrote *The Winter's Tale* that year.

Read, or Not Read

From *Between the Acts, 1941* | Virginia Woolf (1882–1941)

[Choosing for the Pageant:]

Of course, there's the whole of English literature to choose from. But how can one choose? Often on a wet day I begin counting up; what I've read; what I haven't read.

Preface

From *Poems, 1920* | Wilfred Owen (1893–1918)

This book is not about heroes. English poetry is not yet fit to speak of them.

Nor is it about deeds or lands, nor anything about glory, honour, might, majesty, dominion or power, except War.

Above all I am not concerned with Poetry.

My subject of it is War, and the pity of War.

The Poetry is in the pity.

Yet these elegies are not to this generation in no sense consolatory. They may be to the next. All the poet can do today is to warn. That is why the true Poets must be truthful.

(If I thought the letter of this book would last, I might have used proper names; but if the spirit of it survives – survives Prussia – my ambition and those names will have achieved themselves fresher fields than Flanders …)

The Writer in the Garret

From *Packing My Library, 2018* | Alberto Manguel (1948–)

Like so many literary creations that begin as strokes of genius and end up as tiresome clichés (Macbeth complaining about the sound and the fury, Don Quixote tilting at windmills) the image of the garret-bound writer was a mere literary creation, born, no doubt, to describe a certain writer at a certain moment, in a long-lost novel or poem. Only later did it become frozen into the commonplace that riddles us today. Writers may snigger or chuckle at this image, but the public (that vast imaginary creation) looks upon it as the truth and feels allowed to make a number of assumptions. For instance, that writers are misanthropic, that writers are creative only in the most uncomfortable conditions, that writers enjoy squalor. And, most important, that poverty is somehow part of a writer's essence. The fact that a book was written 'in bed in a garret' or that it was 'begun, continued, and ended, under a long course of physic, and a great want of money,' as Jonathan Swift declared in his preface to *A Tale of a Tub*, does not say much about the excellence of the book itself.

The Circumstances of the Author

From *A Tale of a Tub: Preface, 1704* | Jonathan Swift (1667–1745)

I hold fit to lay down this general maxim: whatever reader desires to
have a thorough comprehension of an author's thoughts, cannot take
a better method, than by putting himself into the circumstances and
postures of life, that the writer was in upon every important passage,
as it flowed from his pen: for this will introduce a parity, and strict
correspondence of ideas, between the reader and the author. Now, to
assist the diligent reader in so delicate an affair, as far as brevity will
permit, I have recollected, that the shrewdest pieces of this treatise
were conceived in bed, in a garret; at other times, for a reason best
known to myself, I thought fit to sharpen my invention with hunger;
and in general, the whole work was begun, continued, and ended,
under a long course of physic, and a great want of money.

A Problem

From *Experiment in Autobiography, 1934* | H. G. Wells (1866–1946)

Prelude (1932)

I require a pleasant well-lit writing room in good air and a comfortable bedroom to sleep in – and, if the mood takes me, to write in – both free from distracting noises and indeed all unexpected disturbances. There should be a secretary or at least a typist within call and out of earshot, and, within reach, an abundant library and the rest of the world all hung accessibly on to that secretary's telephone. (But it would have to be a one-way telephone, so that when we wanted news we could ask for it, and when we were not in a state to receive and digest news, we should not have it forced upon us.) That would be the central cell of my life.

That would give the immediate material conditions for the best work possible. I think I would like that the beautiful scenery outside the big windows should be changed ever and again, but I recognize the difficulties in the way of that. In the background there would have to be, at need, food, exercise and stimulating, agreeable and various conversation, and, pervading all my consciousness, there should be a sense of security and attention, an assurance that what was produced, when I had done my best upon it, would be properly significant and effective. In such circumstances I feel I could still do much in these years before me, without hurry and without waste.

The Leisure and Tranquillity of a Library

From *Pride and Prejudice, 1813* | Jane Austen (1775–1817)

Lydia's intention of walking to Meryton was not forgotten; every sister except Mary agreed to go with her; and Mr Collins was to attend them, at the request of Mr Bennet, who was most anxious to get rid of him, and have his library to himself; for thither Mr Collins had followed him after breakfast, and there he would continue, nominally engaged with one of the largest folios in the collection, but really talking to Mr Bennet, with little cessation, of his house and garden at Hunsford. Such doings discomposed Mr Bennet exceedingly. In his library he had been always sure of leisure and tranquillity; and though prepared, as he told Elizabeth, to meet with folly and conceit in every other room in the house, he was used to be free from them there; his civility, therefore, was most prompt in inviting Mr Collins to join his daughters in their walk; and Mr Collins, being in fact much better fitted for a walker than a reader, was extremely well pleased to close his large book, and go.

Books and a Parrot

From *The Remoulding of Groby Lington, 1912*

Saki / H. H. Munro (1870–1916)

In the morning-room of his sister-in-law's house Groby Lington
fidgeted away the passing minutes with the demure restlessness of
advanced middle age. About a quarter of an hour would have to
elapse before it would be time to say his good-byes and make his
way across the village green to the station, with a selected escort of
nephews and nieces. He was a good-natured, kindly dispositioned
man, and in theory he was delighted to pay periodical visits to
the wife and children of his dead brother William; in practice, he
infinitely preferred the comfort and seclusion of his own house and
garden, and the companionship of his books and his parrot to these
rather meaningless and tiresome incursions into a family circle with
which he had little in common.

The Libraries of Heaven

Robert Leighton (1611–1684)

I cannot think the glorious world of mind,
    Embalm'd in books, which I can only see
In patches, though I read my moments blind,
        Is to be lost to me.

I have a thought that, as we live elsewhere,
    So will those dear creations of the brain;
That what I lose unread, I'll find, and there
        Take up my joy again.

O then the bliss of blisses, to be freed
    From all the wants by which the world is driven;
With liberty and endless time to read
        The libraries of Heaven!

Enchantment

From *I Know Why the Caged Bird Sings*, 1969

Maya Angelou (1928–2014)

When I had finished the cookies she brushed off the table and brought a thick small book from the bookcase. I had read *A Tale of Two Cities* and found it up to my standards as a romantic novel. She opened the first page and I heard poetry for the first time in my life.

'It was the best of times and the worst of times ...' Her voice slid in and curved down through and over the words. She was nearly singing. I wanted to look at the pages. Were they the same that I had read? Or were there notes, music, lined on the pages, as in a hymn book? Her sounds began cascading gently. I knew from listening to a thousand preachers that she was nearing the end of her reading, and I hadn't really heard, heard to understand, a single word.

'How do you like that?'

It occurred to me that she expected a response. The sweet vanilla flavour was still on my tongue and her reading was a wonder in my ears. I had to speak.

I said 'Yes ma'am.' It was the least I could do, but the most also.

'There's one more thing. Take this book of poems and memorize one for me. Next time you pay me a visit, I want you to recite.'

I have tried often to search behind the sophistication of years for the enchantment I so easily found in those gifts. The essence escapes but its aura remains. To be allowed, no, invited, into the private lives of strangers, and to share their joys and fears, was a chance to exchange the Southern bitter wormwood for a cup of mead with Beowulf or a hot cup of tea and milk with Oliver Twist. When I said aloud, 'It is a far, far better thing that I do, than I have ever done ...' tears of love filled my eyes at my selflessness.

First Lines

From *A Tale of Two Cities, 1859* | Charles Dickens (1812–1870)

It was the best of times, it was the worst of times, it was the age of wisdom, it was the age of foolishness, it was the epoch of belief, it was the epoch of incredulity, it was the season of Light, it was the season of Darkness, it was the spring of hope, it was the winter of despair, we had everything before us, we had nothing before us, we were all going direct to Heaven, we were all going direct the other way – in short, the period was so far like the present period, that some of its noisiest authorities insisted on it being received, for good or for evil, in the superlative degree of comparison only.

There were a king with a large jaw and a queen with a plain face, on the throne of England; there were a king with a large jaw and a queen with a fair face, on the throne of France. In both countries it was clearer than crystal to the lords of the State preserves of loaves and fishes, that things in general were settled for ever.

It was the year of Our Lord one thousand seven hundred and seventy-five.

William Morris: Country and Town

From *A Literary Pilgrim in England, 1917*

Edward Thomas (1878–1917)

A Cockney was what he tended to prefer calling himself, as a citizen working in the town which was once 'London small and white and clean.' As an artist he preferred to think of such a London, and he achieved it by looking back in *The Earthly Paradise*, and forward in *News from Nowhere*. But the union was an imperfect one. For most of his life he was a somewhat dismayed countryman, but an imperfect Londoner. Probably he was one of those survivors who cannot accept the distinction and division between town and country which has been sharpening ever since

> 'London was a grey-walled town,
> And slow the pack-horse made his way
> Across the curlew-haunted down.'

He passed from one to the other easily. In both he worked and met his friends, artists and Socialists.

No man yet has made a perfect harmony of the two, town and country, and we know nothing about the angels. A man at least has done very well who, either on the Oxfordshire or the Middlesex shore, wrote two or three kinds of poetry and prose, lectured, organized societies and movements, designed wallpaper and chintz, wove tapestry and got others to weave it, dyed and experimented in dyeing, managed a business and kept a shop, was a public examiner and an adviser to a museum, refused the laureateship, caught perch and jack, cooked admirably, and had times when he was 'too happy to think that there could be much amiss anywhere.'

The Kelmscott Press

From *A Note by William Morris on his Aims in Founding the Kelmscott Press, 1896* | William Morris (1834–1896)

I began printing books with the hope of producing some which would have a definite claim to beauty, while at the same time they should be easy to read and should not dazzle the eye, or trouble the intellect of the reader by eccentricity of form in the letters. I have always been a great admirer of the calligraphy of the Middle Ages, and of the earlier printing which took its place. As to the fifteenth-century books, I had noticed that they were always beautiful by force of the mere typography, even without the added ornament, with which many of them are so lavishly supplied. And it was the essence of my undertaking to produce books which it would be a pleasure to look upon as pieces of printing and arrangement of type.

. . . .

It was only natural that I, a decorator by profession, should attempt to ornament my books suitably: about this matter, I will only say that I have always tried to keep in mind the necessity for making my decoration a part of the page of type. I may add that in designing the magnificent and inimitable woodcuts which have adorned several of my books, and will above all adorn the Chaucer which is now drawing near completion, my friend Sir Edward Burne-Jones has never lost sight of this important point, so that his work will not only give us a series of most beautiful and imaginative pictures, but form the most harmonious decoration possible to the printed book.

How to Approach a Book

From *The Secret Life of Books, 2019* | Tom Mole (1976–)

As objects, books are constantly sending us messages about how we should approach the texts they contain. Weighty hardbacks printed on thick paper with sober covers tell us to take them seriously. They are designed to last, allowing their text to be read many times. Detective stories printed on cheap paper with flimsy bindings and garish covers shout at us to buy them, read them fast, and throw them away. If you try to reread them more than a couple of times they will literally fall to pieces. Poetry volumes surround a well-turned sonnet with acres of white margin, like a piece of polished jet displayed on an ample white cushion. The page layout entreats us to bring to the poem a mind cleared of distractions, like the page, and focused tightly on the words islanded in a sea of white paper. When you read a book, you're always reading a material object as well as a string of text. Reading matter always takes the form of, well, matter.

22 November

Victorians: Macaulay and Huxley

From *The Victorian Age in Literature, 1913*

G. K. Chesterton (1874–1936)

If we take Macaulay at the beginning of the epoch and Huxley at the end of it, we shall find that they had much in common. They were both square-jawed, simple men, greedy of controversy but scornful of sophistry, dead to mysticism but very much alive to morality; and they were both very much more under the influence of their own admirable rhetoric than they knew. Huxley, especially, was much more a literary than a scientific man. It is amusing to note that when Huxley was charged with being rhetorical, he expressed his horror of 'plastering the fair face of truth with that pestilent cosmetic, rhetoric', which is itself about as well-plastered a piece of rhetoric as Ruskin himself could have managed. The difference that the period had developed can best be seen if we consider this: that while neither was of a spiritual sort, Macaulay took it for granted that common sense required some kind of theology, while Huxley took it for granted that common sense meant having none. Macaulay, it is said, never talked about his religion: but Huxley was always talking about the religion he hadn't got.

Poets and Poetry

From *Essay on Milton, Edinburgh Review, 1825*

Thomas Babington Macaulay (1800–1859)

Perhaps no person can be a poet, or can even enjoy poetry, without
a certain unsoundness of mind, if anything which gives so much
pleasure ought to be called unsoundness. By poetry we mean not
all writing in verse, nor even all good writing in verse. Our definition
excludes many metrical compositions which, on other grounds,
deserve the highest praise. By poetry we mean the art of employing
words in such a manner as to produce an illusion on the imagination,
the art of doing by means of words what the painter does by
means of colours.

24 November

The Lunatic, the Lover and the Poet

From *A Midsummer Night's Dream*, 1595/6

William Shakespeare (1564–1616)

Act V, scene i, lines 7–21

I never may believe
These antique fables, nor these fairy toys.
Lovers and madmen have such seething brains,
Such shaping fantasies, that apprehend
More than cool reason ever comprehends.
The lunatic, the lover and the poet
Are of imagination all compact:
One sees more devils than vast hell can hold,
That is, the madman: the lover, all as frantic,
Sees Helen's beauty in a brow of Egypt:
The poet's eye, in fine frenzy rolling,
Doth glance from heaven to earth, from earth to heaven;
And as imagination bodies forth
The forms of things unknown, the poet's pen
Turns them to shapes and gives to airy nothing
A local habitation and a name.
Such tricks hath strong imagination,
That if it would but apprehend some joy,
It comprehends some bringer of that joy;
Or in the night, imagining some fear,
How easy is a bush supposed a bear!

For the Dedication of the New City Library, Boston

Oliver Wendell Holmes (1809–1894)

November 26, 1888

Verses 1–8

Proudly, beneath her glittering dome,
　　Our three-hilled city greets the morn;
Here Freedom found her virgin home, –
　　The Bethlehem where her babe was born.

The lordly roofs of traffic rise
　　Amid the smoke of household fires;
High o'er them in the peaceful skies
　　Faith points to heaven her clustering spires.

Can Freedom breathe if ignorance reign?
　　Shall Commerce thrive where anarchs rule?
Will Faith her half-fledged brood retain
　　If darkening counsels cloud the school?

Let in the light! from every age
　　Some gleams of garnered wisdom pour,
And, fixed on thought's electric page,
　　Wait all their radiance to restore.

Let in the light! in diamond mines
    Their gems invite the hand that delves;
So learning's treasured jewels shine
    Ranged on the alcove's ordered shelves.

From history's scroll the splendor streams,
    From science leaps the living ray;
Flashed from the poet's glowing dreams
    The opal fires of fancy play.

Let in the light! these windowed walls
    Shall brook no shadowing colonnades,
But day shall flood the silent halls
    Till o'er yon hills the sunset fades.

Behind the ever open gate
    No pikes shall fence a crumbling throne,
No lackeys cringe, no courtiers wait,
    This palace is the people's own!

Give Me a Highwayman

From *Memories and Portraits, 1904*

Robert Louis Stevenson (1850–1894)

In anything fit to be called by the name of reading, the process itself should be absorbing and voluptuous; we should gloat over a book, be rapt clean out of ourselves, and rise from our perusal, our mind filled with the busiest, kaleidoscopic dance of images, incapable of sleep or continuous thought. The words, if the book be eloquent, should run thenceforward in our ears like the noise of breakers, and the story, if it be a story, repeat itself in a thousand coloured picture to the eye. It was for this last pleasure that we read so closely, and loved our books so dearly, in the bright, troubled period of boyhood. Eloquence and thought, character and conversation, were but obstacles to brush aside as we dug blithely after a certain sort of incident, like a pig for truffles. For my part, I liked a story to begin with an old wayside inn where, 'towards the close of the year 17–', several gentlemen in three-cocked hats were playing bowls. A friend of mine preferred the Malabar coast in a storm, with a ship beating to windward, and a scowling fellow of Herculean proportions striding along the beach; he, to be sure, was a pirate. This was further afield than my home-keeping fancy loved to travel, and designed altogether for a larger canvas than the tales that I affected. Give me a highwayman and I was full to the brim; a Jacobite would do, but the highwayman was my favourite dish.

Windy Nights

Robert Louis Stevenson (1850–1894)

Whenever the moon and stars are set,
   Whenever the wind is high,
All night long in the dark and wet,
   A man goes riding by.
Late in the night when the fires are out,
Why does he gallop and gallop about?

Whenever the trees are crying aloud,
   And ships are tossed at sea,
By, on the highway, low and loud,
   By at the gallop goes he.
By at the gallop he goes, and then
By he comes back at the gallop again.

First Lines

From *Paul Clifford, 1830* | Edward Bulwer-Lytton (1803–1873)

It was a dark and stormy night; the rain fell in torrents – except at occasional intervals, when it was checked by a violent gust of wind which swept up the streets (for it is in London that our scene lies), rattling along the house-tops, and fiercely agitating the scanty flame of the lamps that struggled against the darkness. Through one of the obscurest quarters of London, and among haunts little loved by the gentlemen of the police, a man, evidently of the lowest orders, was wending his solitary way.

Taking Fiction Seriously

From *Partial Portraits: Art of Fiction, written 1884, published 1888* | Henry James (1843–1916)

It must take itself seriously for the public to take it so. The old superstition about fiction being 'wicked' has doubtless died out in England; but the spirit of it lingers in a certain oblique regard directed toward any story which does not more or less admit that it is only a joke. Even the most jocular novel feels in some degree the weight of the proscription that was formerly directed against literary levity: the jocularity does not always succeed in passing for orthodoxy. It is still expected, though perhaps people are ashamed to say it, that a production which is after all only a 'make-believe' (for what else is a 'story'?) shall be in some degree apologetic – shall renounce the pretension of attempting really to represent life.

30 November

DECEMBER

The Craft of Genius

Poet

Ralph Waldo Emerson (1803–1882)

To clothe the fiery thought
In simple words succeeds,
For still the craft of genius is
To mask a king in weeds.

Jane Austen

From *The Victorian Age in Literature, 1913*

G. K. Chesterton (1874–1936)

No woman later has captured the complete common sense of Jane Austen. She could keep her head, while all the after women went about looking for their brains. She could describe a man coolly; which neither George Eliot nor Charlotte Brontë could do. She knew what she knew, like a sound dogmatist: she did not know what she did not know – like a sound agnostic.

No Enjoyment Like Reading

From *Pride and Prejudice, 1813* | Jane Austen (1775–1817)

[Darcy took up a book; Miss Bingley did the same.]

Miss Bingley's attention was quite as much engaged in watching
Mr. Darcy's progress through *his* book, as in reading her own;
and she was perpetually either making some inquiry, or looking
at his page. She could not win him, however, to any conversation;
he merely answered her question, and read on. At length, quite
exhausted by the attempt to be amused with her own book, which
she had only chosen because it was the second volume of his, she gave
a great yawn and said: 'How pleasant it is to spend an evening in this
way! I declare after all there is no enjoyment like reading! How much
sooner one tires of anything than of a book! – When I have a house
of my own, I shall be miserable if I have not an excellent library.'

No one made any reply. She then yawned again, threw aside her
book, and cast her eyes round the room in quest of some amusement.

Bookcases

From *The Private Library, 1897* | A. L. Humphreys (1865–1946)

Junior Assistant and later Partner, Hatchards Bookshop (1881–1924)

The chief faults of bookcases arise from their being designed and made by men who have never used a book. A first requisite in bookcases is simplicity, bearing in mind that the books are the ornament and not the bookcases. The cabinet-maker, among other things, is too fond of embellishments, and sacrifices space to what seem odd angularities and irregularities.

No bookcase should be above eight and a half feet in height. No ladder should be necessary to get at books. If books are 'skied' up to the ceiling they must suffer from the heated air. It is heat, not gas merely, which damages books.

A room may be made to look very beautiful by being surrounded with fumed oak bookcases, eight feet high.

. . . .

In estimating the extent of shelving which it may be necessary to provide, we may calculate that in an ordinary library a space two feet high and two feet wide will, on an average, contain about thirty-five volumes, and it may be estimated roughly that every thousand volumes in a library will require about a hundred square feet of shelving.

The Non-Reading of Books

From *Unpacking My Library, 1931* | Walter Benjamin (1892–1940)

The non-reading of books, you will object, should be characteristic
of collectors? This is news to me, you may say. It is not news at all.
Experts will bear me out when I say that it is the oldest thing in
the world. Suffice it to quote the answer which Anatole France gave
to a philistine who admired his library and then finished with the
standard question, 'And have you read all these books, Monsieur
France?' 'Not one-tenth of them. I don't suppose you use your
Sèvres china every day?'

5 December

Read What You Want

From *The Complete Polysyllabic Spree, 2006* | Nick Hornby (1957–)

Reading for enjoyment is what we all should be doing. I don't mean
we should all be reading chick-lit or thrillers (although if that's what
you want to read, it's fine by me, because here's something no one
else will ever tell you: if you don't read the classics, or the novel
that won this year's Booker Prize, then *nothing bad will happen to
you*; more importantly, *nothing good will happen to you if you do*);
I simply mean that turning pages should not be like walking through
thick mud. The whole purpose of books is that we read them, and if
you find you can't, it might not be your inadequacy that's to blame.
'Good' books can be pretty awful sometimes.

To Read Well

From *Walden; or, Life in the Woods, 1854*

Henry David Thoreau (1817–1862)

To read well – that is, to read true books in a true spirit – is a noble
exercise, and one that will task the reader more than any exercise
which the customs of the day esteem. It requires a training such as
the athletes underwent, the steady intention almost of the whole
life to this object. Books must be read as deliberately and reservedly
as they were written. It is not enough even to be able to speak the
language of that nation by which they are written, for there is a
memorable interval between the spoken and the written language,
the language heard and the language read. The one is commonly
transitory – a sound, a tongue, a dialect merely, almost brutish, and
we learn it unconsciously, like the brutes, of our mothers. The other
is the maturity and experience of that: if that is our mother tongue,
this is our father tongue, a reserved and select expression,
too significant to be heard by the ear, which we must be born again
in order to speak.

7 December

Desperate Reading

From *Of Time and the River*, 1935 | Thomas Wolfe (1900–1938)

Book II, Young Faustus VII

Now he would prowl the stacks of the library at night, pulling books out of a thousand shelves and reading in them like a madman. The thought of these vast stacks of books would drive him mad: the more he read, the less he seemed to know – the greater the number of the books he read, the greater the immense uncountable number of those which he could never read would seem to be. Within a period of ten years he read at least 20,000 volumes – deliberately the number is set low – and opened the pages and looked through many times that number. This may seem unbelievable, but it happened. Dryden said this about Ben Jonson: 'Other men read books, but he read libraries' – and so now was it with this boy. Yet this terrific orgy of the books brought him no comfort, peace, or wisdom of the mind and heart. Instead, his fury and despair increased from what they fed upon, his hunger mounted with the food it ate.

He read insanely, by the hundreds, the thousands, the ten thousands, yet he had no desire to be bookish; no one could describe this mad assault upon print as scholarly: a ravening appetite to him demanded that he read everything that had ever been written about human experience. He read no more from pleasure – the thought that other books were waiting for him tore at his heart for ever.

. . . .

This fury which drove him on to read so many books had nothing to do with scholarship, nothing to do with academic honours, nothing to do with formal learning. He was not in any way a scholar and did not want to be one. He simply wanted to know about everything on earth; he wanted to devour the earth, and it drove him mad when he saw he could not do this.

Thomas Hobbes

From *Brief Lives, 1669–1696* | John Aubrey (1626–1697)

He thought much and with excellent method and stedinesse, which made him seldome make a false step.

His books. He had very few bookes. I never sawe (nor Sir William Petty) above halfe a dozen about him in his chamber. Homer and Virgil were commonly on his table; sometimes Xenophon, or some probable historie, and Greek Testament, or so.

Reading. He had read much, if one considers his long life; but his contemplation was much more then his reading. He was wont to say that if he had read as much as other men, he should have knowne no more then other men.

Picture-Books in Winter

Robert Louis Stevenson (1850–1894)

Summer fading, winter comes –
Frosty mornings, tingling thumbs
Window robins, winter rooks,
And the picture story-books.

Water now is turned to stone
Nurse and I can walk upon;
Still we find the flowing brooks
In the picture story-books.

All the pretty things put by,
Wait upon the children's eye,
Sheep and shepherds, trees and crooks,
In the picture story-books.

We may see how all things are,
Seas and cities, near and far,
And the flying fairies' looks,
In the picture story-books.

How am I to sing your praise,
Happy chimney-corner days,
Sitting safe in nursery nooks,
Reading picture story-books?

New Books

From *On Reading New Books, Florence, May 1825*

William Hazlitt (1778–1830)

I cannot understand the rage manifested by the greater part of the world for reading New Books. If the public had read all those that have gone before, I can conceive how they should not wish to read the same work twice over but when I consider the countless volumes that lie unopened, unregarded, unread, and unthought-of, I cannot enter into the pathetic complaints that I hear made that Sir Walter writes no more – that the press is idle – that Lord Byron is dead. If I have not read a book before, it is, to all intents and purposes, new to me, whether it was printed yesterday or three hundred years ago. If it be urged that it has no modern, passing incidents, and is out of date and old-fashioned, then it is so much the newer; it is farther removed from other works that I have lately read, from the familiar routine of ordinary life, and makes so much more addition to my knowledge. But many people would as soon think of putting on old armour as of taking up a book not published within the last month, or year at the utmost. There is a fashion in reading as well as in dress, which lasts only for the season.

New and Ancient Books

From *Letters from a Citizen of the World to his Friends in the East, 1760–1761* | Oliver Goldsmith (1728–1774)

Extract: Letter LXXIV

From Lien Chi Altangi to Fum Hoam, First President of the Ceremonial Academy at Pekin, in China

There are numbers in this city who live by writing new books; and yet there are thousands of volumes in every large library unread and forgotten. This, upon my arrival, was one of those contradictions which I was unable to account for. 'Is it possible,' said I, 'that there should be any demand for new books, before those already published are read? Can there be so many employed in producing a commodity with which the market is already over-stocked; and with goods also better than any of modern manufacture?'

What at first view appeared an inconsistence, is a proof at once of this people's wisdom and refinement. Even allowing the works of their ancestors better written than theirs, yet those of the moderns acquire a real value, by being marked with the impression of the times. Antiquity has been in the possession of others; the present is our own: let us first therefore learn to know what belongs to ourselves, and then, if we have leisure, cast our reflections back to the reign of Shonou, who governed twenty thousand years before the creation of the moon.

Modern Rhymes

From *An Essay on Criticism, 1709* | Alexander Pope (1688–1744)

Lines 474–493

Be thou the first true merit to befriend;
His praise is lost, who stays, till all commend.
Short is the date, alas, of modern rhymes,
And 'tis but just to let them live betimes.
No longer now that golden age appears,
When Patriarch-wits surviv'd a thousand years:
Now length of Fame (our second life) is lost,
And bare threescore is all ev'n that can boast;
Our sons their fathers' failing language see,
And such as Chaucer is, shall Dryden be.
So when the faithful pencil has design'd
Some bright idea of the master's mind,
Where a new world leaps out at his command,
And ready Nature waits upon his hand;
When the ripe colours soften and unite,
And sweetly melt into just shade and light;
When mellowing years their full perfection give,
And each bold figure just begins to live,
The treach'rous colours the fair art betray,
And all the bright creation fades away!

Talking to Books

From *The Interesting Narrative of the Life of Olaudah Equiano, 1789* | Olaudah Equiano (c. 1745–1797)

[Olaudah Equiano could read well but hoped to show the reader that he always strived to better himself.]

I had often seen my master and Dick employed in reading; and I had a great curiosity to talk to the books, as I thought they did; and so to learn how all things had a beginning: for that purpose I have so often taken up a book, and have talked to it, and then put my ears to it, when alone, in hopes it would answer me; and I have been very much concerned when I found it remained silent.

To the Reader

Ben Jonson (1572–1637)

Pray thee, take care, that tak'st my booke in hand,
To reade it well: that is, to understand.

A Prophesy

From *The Moonstone, 1868* | Wilkie Collins (1824–1889)

[Gabriel Betteridge is asked by Mr Franklin to tell his part of the story of the Indian Diamond or Moonstone.]

In the first part of *Robinson Crusoe*, at page one hundred and twenty-nine, you will find it thus written:

'Now I saw, though too late, the Folly of beginning a Work before we count the Cost, and before we judge rightly of our own Strength to go through with it.'

Only yesterday, I opened my *Robinson Crusoe* at that place.

. . . .

Two hours have passed since Mr. Franklin left me. As soon as his back was turned, I went to my writing-desk to start the story. There I have sat helpless (in spite of my abilities) ever since; seeing what Robinson Crusoe saw, as quoted above – namely, the folly of beginning a work before we count the cost, and before we judge rightly of our own strength to go through with it. Please to remember, I opened the book by accident, at that bit, only the day before I rashly undertook the business now in hand; and, allow me to ask – if that isn't prophecy, what is?

I am not superstitious; I have read a heap of books in my time, I am a scholar in my own way. Though turned seventy, I possess an active memory, and legs to correspond. You are not to take it, if you please, as the saying of an ignorant man, when I express my opinion that such a book as *Robinson Crusoe* never was written, and never will be written again. I have tried that book for years – generally in combination with a pipe of tobacco – and I have found it my friend in need in all the necessities of this mortal life. When my spirits are bad – *Robinson Crusoe*. When I want advice – *Robinson Crusoe*. In past times, when my wife plagued me; in present times, when I have had a drop too much – *Robinson Crusoe*.

I have worn out six stout *Robinson Crusoes* with hard work in my service. On my lady's last birthday she gave me a seventh. I took a drop too much on the strength of it; and *Robinson Crusoe* put me right again. Price four shillings and sixpence, bound in blue, with a picture into the bargain.

Still, this don't look much like starting the story of the Diamond – does it? I seem to be wandering off in search of Lord knows what. Lord knows where. We will take a new sheet of paper, if you please, and begin over again, with my best respects to you.

Organisation

From *Diary* | Samuel Pepys (1633–1703)

Dec. 17, 1666

Spent the evening in fitting my books, to have the number set upon
each, in order to my having an alphabet of my whole, which will be
of great ease to me. This day Captain Batters come from sea in his
fireship and come to see me, poor man, as his patron, and a poor
painful wretch he is as can be. After supper to bed.

Dec. 19, 1666

Home full of trouble on these considerations, and, among other
things, I to my chamber, and there to ticket a good part of my books,
in order to the numbering of them for my easy finding them to read
as I have occasion.

Jan. 8, 1667

So home and to supper, and then saw the catalogue of my books,
which my brother had wrote out, now perfectly alphabeticall, and
so to bed.

Feb. 4, 1666–67

Mightily pleased with the play, we home by coach, and there a
little to the office, and then to my chamber, and there finished my
catalogue of my books with my own hand, and so to supper and to
bed, and had a good night's rest, the last night's being troublesome,
but now my heart light and full of resolution of standing close to
my business.

Sonnet LXXVI

William Shakespeare (1564–1616)

Why is my verse so barren of new pride,
So far from variation or quick change?
Why with the time do I not glance aside
To new-found methods, and to compounds strange?
Why write I still all one, ever the same,
And keep invention in a noted weed,
That every word doth almost tell my name,
Showing their birth, and where they did proceed?
O know, sweet love, I always write of you,
And you and love are still my argument:
So all my best is dressing old words new,
Spending again what is already spent:
    For as the sun is daily new and old,
      So is my love still telling what is told.

Barcelona

From *Dear Howard, 2018* | David Batterham (1933–)

19 December 1990
Thursday. A mixed day's shopping. My best buy is a treatise
with coloured photographs on sexually transmitted skin diseases.
Unsaleable of course.

And a little catalogue with socks and stockings with hairy
engravings. Could be a Dada novella.

A project by M. de Lesseps for building a canal through the
Isthme de Suez 1855 is more promising. In fact I will try to make
it pay for my airfare.

A small pile of 1920s hairdressing magazines is just worth having.
Most reckless was a book by Eluard with woodcuts by Miró, which
was suspiciously cheap.

Eastern Tales and Oriental Histories

From *Letters from a Citizen of the World to his Friends in the East, 1760–1761* | Oliver Goldsmith (1728–1774)

Extract: Letter XXXII

From Lien Chi Altangi to Fum Hoam, First President of the Ceremonial Academy at Pekin, in China

I yesterday received an invitation from a lady of distinction, who it seems had collected all her knowledge of Eastern manner from fictions every day propagated here, under the titles of Eastern tales and Oriental histories; she received me very politely, but seemed to wonder that I neglected bringing opium and a tobacco-box; when chairs were drawn for the rest of the company, I was assigned my place on a cushion on the floor. It was in vain that I protested the Chinese used chairs as in Europe: she understood decorum too well to entertain me with the ordinary civilities.

The Strand Bookstore

From *Dash and Lily's Book of Dares, 2010* | David Levithan (1972–)
Rachel Cohn (1968–)

Dash, December 21st

Mostly I was spending time in the Strand, that bastion of titillating
erudition, not so much a bookstore but the collision of a hundred
different bookstores with literary wreckage strewn over eighteen
miles of shelves. All the clerks there counter-slouch around
distractedly in their skinny jeans and their thrift-store button-downs,
like older siblings who will never, ever be bothered to talk to you or
care about you or even acknowledge your existence if their friends
are around … which they always are. Some bookstores want you to
believe they're a community center, like they need to host a cookie-
making class in order to sell you some Proust. But the Strand leaves
you completely on your own, caught between the warring forces of
organization and idiosyncrasy, with idiosyncrasy winning every time.
In other words, it was my kind of graveyard.

I was usually in the mood to look for nothing in particular when
I went to the Strand. Some days, I would decide that the afternoon
was sponsored by a particular letter, and would visit each and every
section to check out the authors whose last name began with that
letter. Other days, I would decide to tackle a single section, or would
investigate the recently unloaded tomes, thrown into bins that never
really conformed to alphabetization. Or maybe I'd only look at books
with green covers, because it had been too long since I'd read a book
with a green cover.

The Symbolic Role of the King's Library

From *The Design and Construction of the British Library,*
1998 | Colin St John Wilson (1922–2007)

In the British Library the symbolic role is most truly embodied in
the King's Library. It was a condition of the gift to the nation of this
great collection of George III that its beautiful leather and vellum
bindings should be on show to the general public and not just to the
scholars. The volumes have hitherto been distributed in the wall-cases
of the British Museum where its identity, however handsome, has the
passive character of decoration to the walls of the space dedicated
to exhibitions. In the new building the collection is housed in a
free-standing structure, an object in its own right, a six-storey-high
bronze and glass tower. By this transformation it becomes
simultaneously a celebration of beautifully bound books, a
towering gesture that announces the invisible presence of treasures
housed below and a hard-working source of material studied in
the Rare Book Reading Room opposite: the symbolic role is at one
with the use.

The Bodleian Library

From *The Life of Sir Thomas Bodley, dated 15 December 1609, published 1647* | Sir Thomas Bodley (1545–1613)

Onely this I muſt truly confeffe of my felfe, that though I did never repent me yet of thofe and fome other my often refufalls of honourable offers, in refpect of enriching my private eflate, yet fomewhat more of late have blamed my felfe, & my nicety that way, for the love that I beare to my Reverend Mother the Univerfity of Oxford, and to the advancement of her good, by fuch kind of means as I have since undertaken. For thus I fell to difcourfe and debate in my mind, that although I might find it fitteft for me, to keep out of the throng of Court contentions, & addreffe my thoughts & deeds to fuch ends altogether, as I my felfe could beft affect; yet withall I was to think, that my duty towards God, the expectation of the world, my naturall inclination, & very morality, did require, that I fhould not wholly fo hide thofe little abilities that I had, but that in fome meafure, in one kind or other, I fhould doe the true part of a profitable member in the State: whereupon examining exactly for the reft of my life, what courfe I might take, and having fought (as I thought, all the waies to the wood) to felect the moft proper, I concluded at the laft to fet up my Staffe at the Library doore in Oxford; being throughly perfwaded, that in my folitude and furceafe from the Common-wealth affaires, I could not bufy my felfe to better purpofe, then by reducing that place (which then in every part lay ruined and waft) to the publique ufe of Students.

Written with my owne hand Anno 1609.

Nailing Things Down

From *The Phoenix: Morality and the Novel, 1936*

D. H. Lawrence (1885–1930)

If you try to nail anything down in the novel, either it kills the novel, or the novel gets up and walks away with the nail.

24 December

Christmas Books

From *Little Women, 1869* | Louisa May Alcott (1832–1888)

Jo was the first to wake in the grey dawn of Christmas morning. No stockings hung at the fireplace, and for a moment she felt as much disappointed as she did long ago, when her little sock fell down because it was so crammed with goodies. Then she remembered her mother's promise, and slipping her hand under her pillow, drew out a little crimson-covered book. She knew it very well, for it was that beautiful old story of the best life ever lived, and Jo felt that it was a true guide-book for any pilgrim going the long journey. She woke Meg with a 'Merry Christmas,' and bade her see what was under her pillow. A green-covered book appeared, with the same picture inside, and a few words written by their mother, which made their one present very precious in their eyes. Presently Beth and Amy woke, to rummage and find their little books also – one dove-coloured, the other blue; and all sat looking at and talking about them, while the east grew rosy with the coming day.

In spite of her small vanities, Margaret had a sweet and pious nature, which unconsciously influenced her sisters, especially Jo, who loved her very tenderly, and obeyed her because her advice was so gently given.

'Girls,' said Meg seriously, looking from the tumbled head beside her to the two little night-capped ones in the room beyond, 'mother wants us to read and love and mind these books, and we must begin at once. We used to be faithful about it; but since father went away, and all this war trouble unsettled us, we have neglected many things. You can do as you please; but I shall keep my book on the table here, and read a little every morning as soon as I wake, for I know it will do me good, and help me through the day.'

The Restricted Section in the Library

From *Harry Potter and the Philosopher's Stone, 1997*

J. K. Rowling (1965–)

[Harry is given his father's Invisibility Cloak. He puts it on and goes exploring.]

Where should he go? He stopped, his heart racing, and thought. And then it came to him. The Restricted Section in the Library. He'd be able to read as long as he liked, as long as it took to find out who Flamel was. He set off, drawing the Invisibility Cloak tight around him as he walked.

The library was pitch black and very eerie. Harry lit a lamp to see his way along a row of books. The lamp looked as if it was floating in mid-air, and even though Harry could feel his arm supporting it, the sight gave him the creeps.

The Restricted Section was right at the back of the library. Stepping carefully over the rope which separated these books from the rest of the library, he held up his lamp to read the titles.

They didn't tell him much. Their peeling, faded gold letters spelled words in languages Harry couldn't understand. Some had no title at all. One book had a dark stain on it that looked horribly like blood. The hairs on the back of Harry's neck prickled. Maybe he was imagining it, maybe not, but he thought a faint whispering was coming from the books, as though they knew someone was there who shouldn't be.

He had to start somewhere. Setting the lamp down carefully on the floor, he looked along the bottom shelf for an interesting-looking book. A large black and silver volume caught his eye. He pulled it out with difficulty, because it was very heavy, and, balancing it on his knee, let it fall open.

A piercing, blood-curdling shriek split the silence – the book was screaming! Harry snapped it shut, but the shriek went on and on, one high, unbroken, ear-splitting note. He stumbled backwards and knocked over his lamp, which went out at once. Panicking, he heard footsteps coming down the corridor outside – stuffing the shrieking book back on the shelf, he ran for it. He passed Filch almost in the doorway; Filch's pale, wild eyes looked straight through him and Harry slipped under Filch's outstretched arm and streaked off up the corridor, the book's shrieks still ringing in his ears.

Novels: Their Foes and Readers

From *Northanger Abbey, 1817* | Jane Austen (1775–1817)

If a rainy morning deprived them [Catherine and Isabella] of other enjoyments, they were still resolute in meeting in defiance of wet and dirt, and shut themselves up to read novels together. Yes, novels; for I will not adopt that ungenerous and impolitic custom, so common with novel-writers, of degrading, by their contemptuous censure, the very performances to the number of which they are themselves adding; joining with their greatest enemies in bellowing the harshest epithets on such works, and scarcely ever permitting them to be read by their own heroine, who, if she accidentally take up a novel, is sure to turn over its insipid pages with disgust. Alas! if the heroine of one novel be not patronised by the heroine of another, from whom can she expect protection and regard? I cannot approve of it. Let us leave it to the reviewers to abuse such effusions of fancy at their leisure, and over every new novel to talk in threadbare strains of the trash with which the press now groans. Let us not desert one another – we are an injured body. Although our productions have afforded more extensive and unaffected pleasure than those of any other literary corporation in the world, no species of composition has been so much decried. From pride, ignorance, or fashion, our foes are almost as many as our readers; and while the abilities of the nine-hundredth abridger of the History of England, or of the man who collects and publishes in a volume some dozen lines of Milton, Pope, and Prior, with a paper from the Spectator and a chapter from Sterne, are eulogised by a thousand pens, – there seems almost a general wish of decrying the capacity and undervaluing the labour of the novelist, and of slighting the performances which have only genius, wit, and taste to recommend them.

The Lexicographer

From *A Dictionary of the English Language: Preface, 1755*

Samuel Johnson (1709–1784)

It is the fate of those who toil at the lower employments of life …
to be exposed to censure, without hope of praise; to be disgraced
by miscarriage, or punished for neglect … Among those unhappy
mortals is the writer of dictionaries … Every other author may aspire
to praise; the lexicographer can only hope to escape reproach.

The Two Sides

From *A Full and True Account of the Battle Fought Last Friday Between the Ancient and Modern Books in Saint James's Library*, 1704 | Jonathan Swift (1667–1745)

They resolved it should come to a battle.

Immediately the two main bodies withdrew, under their several ensigns, to the farther parts of the library, and there entered into cabals and consults upon the present emergency. The moderns were in very warm debates upon the choice of their leaders; and nothing less than the fear impending from their enemies could have kept them from mutinies upon this occasion. The difference was greatest among the horse, where every private trooper pretended to the chief command, from Tasso and Milton to Dryden and Withers. The light-horse were commanded by Cowley and Despreaux. There came the bowmen under their valiant leaders, Des Cartes, Gassendi, and Hobbes; whose strength was such that they could shoot their arrows beyond the atmosphere, never to fall down again, but turn, like that of Evander, into meteors; or, like the cannon-ball, into stars. Paracelsus brought a squadron of stinkpot-flingers from the snowy mountains at Rhætia. There came vast body of dragoons, of different nations, under the leading of Harvey, their great aga: part armed with scythes, the weapons of death; part with lances and long knives, all steeped in poison; part shot bullets of a most malignant nature, and used white powder which infallibly killed without report. There came several bodies of heavy-armed foot, all mercenaries, under the ensigns of Guicciardini, Davila, Polydore Virgil, Buchanan, Mariana, Camden, and others. The engineers were commanded by Regiomontanus and Wilkins. The rest was a confused multitude, led by Scotus, Aquinas, and Bellarmine; of mighty bulk and stature, but without either arms, courage, or discipline. In the last place came infinite swarms of calones, a disorderly rout led by L'Estrange; rogues and ragamuffins, that follow the camp for nothing but the plunder, all without coats to cover them.

The army of the ancients was much fewer in number; Homer led the horse, and Pindar the lighthorse; Euclid was chief engineer; Plato and Aristotle commanded the bowmen; Herodotus and Livy the foot; Hippocrates, the dragoons; the allies, led by Vossius and Temple, brought up the rear.

Literature Suited to Desolate Islands

From *A Fable for Critics, 1848* | James Russell Lowell (1819–1891)

Lines 474–485

I've thought very often't would be a good thing
In all public collections of books, if a wing
Were set off by itself, like the seas from the dry lands,
Marked *Literature suited to desolate islands*,
And filled with such books as could never be read
Save by readers of proofs, forced to do it for bread, –
Such books as one's wrecked on in small country-taverns,
Such as hermits might mortify over in caverns,
Such as Satan, if printing had then been invented,
As the climax of woe, would to Job have presented,
Such as Crusoe might dip in, although there are few so
Outrageously cornered by fate as poor Crusoe.

Finally

My aim has been that the pieces in this collection will act as a starting point for readers. For various reasons these stories could not be included in the anthology; all take books as their starting points, either in the present day, in historical times or in worlds which are slightly different to ours.

Writers, readers and their stories:
  Max Beerbohm, *Seven Men*
  Italo Calvino, *If on a Winter's Night a Traveller*
  Elena Ferrante, *My Brilliant Friend*
  David Foenkinos, *The Mystery of Henri Pick*
  Diane Setterfield, *The Thirteenth Tale*
  Eley Williams, *The Liar's Dictionary*
  Pip Williams, *The Dictionary of Lost Words*

Booksellers, fantastical and real:
  Kerri Maher, *The Paris Bookseller*
  Garth Nix, *The Left-Handed Booksellers of London*
  Christopher Morley, *Parnassus on Wheels, The Haunted Bookshop*
  Louise Erdrich, *The Sentence*

Librarians and their stories:
  Antonio Iturbe, *The Librarian of Auschwitz*
  Stephen King, *The Library Policeman*
  Janet Skeslien Charles, *The Paris Library*
  Salley Vickers, *The Librarian*

People who want to save or destroy books:
  Ray Bradbury, *Fahrenheit 451*
  Geraldine Brooks, *People of the Book*
  Robert Marshall-Andrews, *The Palace of Wisdom*
  Dai Sijie, *Balzac and the Little Chinese Seamstress*

Literary mysteries and murders:

Laurence Cossé, *The Novel Bookstore*

Umberto Eco, *The Name of the Rose*

Claude Izner, *Murder on the Eiffel Tower*

Antoine Laurain, *The Readers' Room*

Charles Palliser, *The Quincunx*

Markus Zusak, *The Book Thief*

Murder by the Book, a selection of short stories edited by
Martin Edwards

Magical books – to some extent, all books are magical, these are
simply more so:

Douglas Adams, *The Hitch-Hiker's Guide to the Galaxy*

Bridget Collins, *The Binding*

Michael Ende, *The Neverending Story*

Elizabeth Kostova, *The Historian*

Erin Morganstern, *The Starless Sea*

Carlos Ruiz Zafón, *The Shadow of the Wind*

Index

432

Sources

John Agard, *My Name is Book: An Autobiography*, text copyright © 2014 John Agard. From MY NAME IS BOOK Written by John Agard and illustrated by Neil Packer. Reproduced by permission of Walker Books Ltd, London, SE11 5HJ www.walker.co.uk.

Maya Angelou, *I Know Why the Caged Bird Sings*. UK rights: copyright © Maya Angelou 1969. Reproduced with permission of the Licensor through PLSClear. North American rights: "Chapter 15" from I KNOW WHY THE CAGED BIRD SINGS by Maya Angelou, copyright © 1969 and renewed 1997 by Maya Angelou. Used by permission of Random House, an imprint and division of Penguin Random House LLC. All rights reserved.

James Baldwin, *Notes of a Native Son*, copyright © The Estate of James Baldwin, Penguin Random House.

David Batterham, *Dear Howard: Tales Told in Letters*, copyright © David Batterham 2018. Reproduced by permission of Redstone Press.

Hilaire Belloc, 'On His Books' and 'On the Gift of a Book to a Child' from *Complete Verse*, Pimlico, 2011, copyright © The Estate of Hilaire Belloc. Peters, Fraser and Dunlop Literary Agents, London.

Walter Benjamin, *Illuminations* published by Jonathan Cape. Copyright © Suhkamp Verlag, Frankfurt Am Main 1955. Reprinted by permission of The Random House Group Limited.

Alan Bennett, *The Uncommon Reader*, copyright © Alan Bennett 2007. Reproduced by permission of Faber and Faber Ltd.

Books on Books

I consulted many books whilst compiling this anthology; these were the most interesting.

Matthew Battles, *Library: An Unquiet History*, William Heinemann, 2003

Matthew Battles, *Palimpsest: A History of the Written Word*, W. W. Norton, 2015

John Carey, *A Little History of Poetry*, Yale University Press, 2020

Ann Fadiman, *Ex Libris*, Penguin Books, 2000

Keith Houston, *The Book*, W. W. Norton & Company, 2016

Ross King, *The Bookseller of Florence*, Chatto & Windus, 2021

Michael Leapman, *The Book of the British Library*, The British Library, 2012

Martyn Lyons, *Books: A Living History*, Thames & Hudson, 2011

Anthony O'Hear, *The Great Books*, Icon Books, 2007

Andrew Pettegree and Arthur der Weduwen, *The Library: A Fragile History*, Profile Books, 2021

Francis Spufford, *The Child that Books Built*, Faber & Faber, 2003

John Sutherland, *A Little History of Literature*, Yale University Press, 2013

Edward Wilson-Lee, *The Catalogue of Shipwrecked Books*, William Collins, 2018